OPPOSING
VIEWPOINTS®
SERIES

D0448092

Identity Politics

Other Books of Related Interest

Opposing Viewpoints Series

Democracy
The Democratic Party
Political Campaigns
The Presidential Election Process
The Republican Party

At Issue Series

Campaign Finance
Does the US Two-Party System Still Work?
Negative Campaigning
The Occupy Movement
Political Activism

Current Controversies Series

The Political Elite and Special Interests
Politics and Media
Politics and Religion
The Tea Party Movement
Women in Politics

> "Congress shall make no law … abridging the freedom of speech, or of the press."
>
> *First Amendment to the US Constitution*

The basic foundation of our democracy is the First Amendment guarantee of freedom of expression. The Opposing Viewpoints series is dedicated to the concept of this basic freedom and the idea that it is more important to practice it than to enshrine it.

Identity Politics

Elizabeth Schmermund, Book Editor

GREENHAVEN PUBLISHING

Published in 2018 by Greenhaven Publishing, LLC
353 3rd Avenue, Suite 255, New York, NY 10010

First Edition

Articles in Greenhaven Publishing anthologies are often edited for length to meet page
requirements. In addition, original titles of these works are changed to clearly present
the main thesis and to explicitly indicate the author's opinion. Every effort is made to
ensure that Greenhaven Publishing accurately reflects the original intent of the authors.
Every effort has been made to trace the owners of the copyrighted material.

Cover image: Tinxi/Shutterstock.com

Library of Congress Cataloging-in-Publication Data

Names: Schmermund, Elizabeth, editor.
Title: Identity politics / Elizabeth Schmermund, book editor.
Description: First edition. | New York : Greenhaven Publishing, [2018] |
  Series: Opposing viewpoints | Audience: Grade 9 to 12. |
Includes bibliographical references and index.
Identifiers: LCCN 2017038061| ISBN 9781534501744
(library bound) | ISBN 9781534501805 (pbk.)
Subjects: LCSH: Political culture—United States—Juvenile literature. |
  Identity politics—United States—Juvenile literature. | Group identity—
Political aspects—United States—Juvenile literature.
Classification: LCC JK1726 .I34 2018 | DDC 306.2—dc23
LC record available at https://lccn.loc.gov/2017038061

Manufactured in the United States of America

Website: http://greenhavenpublishing.com

Contents

Chapter 1: How Has Identity Politics Historically Shaped Policy and Law?

Chapter 2: How Has Identity Politics Incorporated or Ignored Intersectionality?

Chapter 3: How Has Identity Politics Ignored Other Useful Ways of Political Organizing?

Chapter 4: How Can Identity Politics Become a More Useful Political Organizing Tool in the Future?

The Importance of Opposing Viewpoints

Perhaps every generation experiences a period in time in which the populace seems especially polarized, starkly divided on the important issues of the day and gravitating toward the far ends of the political spectrum and away from a consensus-facilitating middle ground. The world that today's students are growing up in and that they will soon enter into as active and engaged citizens is deeply fragmented in just this way. Issues relating to terrorism, immigration, women's rights, minority rights, race relations, health care, taxation, wealth and poverty, the environment, policing, military intervention, the proper role of government—in some ways, perennial issues that are freshly and uniquely urgent and vital with each new generation—are currently roiling the world.

If we are to foster a knowledgeable, responsible, active, and engaged citizenry among today's youth, we must provide them with the intellectual, interpretive, and critical-thinking tools and experience necessary to make sense of the world around them and of the all-important debates and arguments that inform it. After all, the outcome of these debates will in large measure determine the future course, prospects, and outcomes of the world and its peoples, particularly its youth. If they are to become successful members of society and productive and informed citizens, students need to learn how to evaluate the strengths and weaknesses of someone else's arguments, how to sift fact from opinion and fallacy, and how to test the relative merits and validity of their own opinions against the known facts and the best possible available information. The landmark series Opposing Viewpoints has been providing students with just such critical-thinking skills and exposure to the debates surrounding society's most urgent contemporary issues for many years, and it continues to serve this essential role with undiminished commitment, care, and rigor.

The key to the series's success in achieving its goal of sharpening students' critical-thinking and analytic skills resides in its title—

Opposing Viewpoints. In every intriguing, compelling, and engaging volume of this series, readers are presented with the widest possible spectrum of distinct viewpoints, expert opinions, and informed argumentation and commentary, supplied by some of today's leading academics, thinkers, analysts, politicians, policy makers, economists, activists, change agents, and advocates. Every opinion and argument anthologized here is presented objectively and accorded respect. There is no editorializing in any introductory text or in the arrangement and order of the pieces. No piece is included as a "straw man," an easy ideological target for cheap point-scoring. As wide and inclusive a range of viewpoints as possible is offered, with no privileging of one particular political ideology or cultural perspective over another. It is left to each individual reader to evaluate the relative merits of each argument—as he or she sees it, and with the use of ever-growing critical-thinking skills—and grapple with his or her own assumptions, beliefs, and perspectives to determine how convincing or successful any given argument is and how the reader's own stance on the issue may be modified or altered in response to it.

This process is facilitated and supported by volume, chapter, and selection introductions that provide readers with the essential context they need to begin engaging with the spotlighted issues, with the debates surrounding them, and with their own perhaps shifting or nascent opinions on them. In addition, guided reading and discussion questions encourage readers to determine the authors' point of view and purpose, interrogate and analyze the various arguments and their rhetoric and structure, evaluate the arguments' strengths and weaknesses, test their claims against available facts and evidence, judge the validity of the reasoning, and bring into clearer, sharper focus the reader's own beliefs and conclusions and how they may differ from or align with those in the collection or those of their classmates.

Research has shown that reading comprehension skills improve dramatically when students are provided with compelling, intriguing, and relevant "discussable" texts. The subject matter of these collections could not be more compelling, intriguing, or urgently relevant to today's students and the world they are poised to inherit. The anthologized articles and the reading and discussion questions that are included with them also provide the basis for stimulating, lively, and passionate classroom debates. Students who are compelled to anticipate objections to their own argument and identify the flaws in those of an opponent read more carefully, think more critically, and steep themselves in relevant context, facts, and information more thoroughly. In short, using discussable text of the kind provided by every single volume in the Opposing Viewpoints series encourages close reading, facilitates reading comprehension, fosters research, strengthens critical thinking, and greatly enlivens and energizes classroom discussion and participation. The entire learning process is deepened, extended, and strengthened.

For all of these reasons, Opposing Viewpoints continues to be exactly the right resource at exactly the right time—when we most need to provide readers with the critical-thinking tools and skills that will not only serve them well in school but also in their careers and their daily lives as decision-making family members, community members, and citizens. This series encourages respectful engagement with and analysis of opposing viewpoints and fosters a resulting increase in the strength and rigor of one's own opinions and stances. As such, it helps make readers "future ready," and that readiness will pay rich dividends for the readers themselves, for the citizenry, for our society, and for the world at large.

Introduction

> *"At the crux of both sides of identity politics is a simple problem: No one wants to get left behind."*
>
> —*"The Battle over Identity Politics, Explained," by German Lopez, Vox, December 2, 2016*

While once the term "identity politics" was a bit esoteric, today it is one that many people in the United States are familiar with. This is because identity politics has once again resurged to become a point of contention and debate in many political conversations. But what is identity politics? Put very simply, identity politics refers to the belief that people who share certain commonalities (such as race, gender, or sexual orientation) can fight together for a common political goal. According to identity politics, these people can be grouped together based on their identities and can organize politically in a more effective way than through party line politics itself.

While some form of identity politics has been around for centuries, the term first surfaced in the 1960s and 1970s. This was when progressive groups organized around their common goals—and were largely successful. For example, in the civil rights movement in the United States, African Americans formed alliances based on the way they had been oppressively treated because of their race. Together, they demanded more civil rights and more equitable treatment and were successful with the passage of the landmark Civil Rights Act of 1964, which outlawed discrimination based on race, religion, gender, or national origin. Similarly, the women's rights movement in the 1960s and 1970s brought diverse groups of women together to fight under the banner of second-wave feminism. The women's rights movement also had many notable successes, including the passage of Title IX in 1972, which made it illegal for women to be denied any educational program or activity (particularly sports) if the program or activity was funded by the federal government. Another landmark win for women's political organizing was *Roe v. Wade*, a Supreme Court decision that made abortion legal in the United States up until the second trimester.

While identity politics has traditionally been associated with the political left, it has also been used as part of a more conservative political process. Unfortunately, identity politics in recent years has been co-opted by the ultra-right white nationalists. White nationalists believe that the United States must be preserved for white men of European descent. They have been vocal about their racist beliefs and have gained a large following. In fact, during the 2016 US presidential election, many commentators remarked that Donald Trump's successful campaign flirted with such white nationalists and preyed upon fears and racist undertones in the general population.

Just as identity politics can be used across the political spectrum, it has been the object of many criticisms from both the right and the left. Marxist commentators, for example, often opine about how identity politics focuses on race to the exclusion of class. For these Marxists, class struggle is the defining point of identity; every other form of self-identification diverts from the true roots of poverty and oppression. For others, identity politics is exclusionary and even laughable. Yet others denounce identity politics for reinforcing differences, or making the boundaries between groups of people more concrete and, thus, less bridgeable. For many critics of identity politics—and even for proponents of identity politics who feel it has been misused—it can be dangerous to believe that our identities are fixed and that we cannot share political affinities even if we don't share identities. According to them, doing this allows us to be divided into "us" and "them"—and that's no way to make a more just and equitable world for all.

The viewpoints in *Identity Politics* (Opposing Viewpoints) examine the complexities of this hot topic, including criticism leveraged on both sides of the political spectrum and the ways in which the right and left have used identity politics to their advantage. Authors present diverse perspectives in chapters titled "How Has Identity Politics Historically Shaped Policy and Law?," "How Has Identity Politics Incorporated or Ignored Intersectionality?," "How Has Identity Politics Ignored Other Useful Ways of Political Organizing?," and "How Can Identity Politics Become a More Useful Political Organizing Tool in the Future?" These viewpoints will encourage you to think more deeply not only about your own identity and its place in the political arena, but also about the role of identity in politics more generally.

OPPOSING
VIEWPOINTS®
SERIES

CHAPTER 1

How Has Identity Politics Historically Shaped Policy and Law?

Chapter Preface

The viewpoints in this chapter examine identity politics through a lens of political and social history. The first viewpoint in this chapter, written by Matthew Yglesias, argues that identity politics is a necessity. In fact, all politics can boil down to identity politics.

However, this standpoint is refuted by the historical examination of the topic by Joan D. Mandle. For Mandle, a professor of sociology and women's studies, identity politics emerges from a particular moment in the women's liberation movement and the civil rights movement. While it may have led to successful political organizing, it has become transformed into a zero-sum game that positions groups of people against one another and solidifies oppressive structures.

Following Mandle's critique of identity politics are discussions of the resurgence of white nationalism, which has recently been rebranded as the "alt-right" movement. White nationalist leaders David Duke and others, such as alt-right movement founder Richard Spencer, have used identity politics to advance a racist ideology that appeals to groups of disaffected and disadvantaged young men like Nathan Benjamin Damigo, an Iraqi War veteran, former Marine, and avowed "identitarian." For identitarians, political organization revolves around race and ethnicity. Identitarians like Damigo feel that they have suffered from the rise of multiculturalism and that they must fight to ensure a place in the world for white men of European descent.

Thus, while identity politics is responsible for many victories in regard to civil liberties, it also has a dark underbelly whereby some groups can actively and unapologetically work for racist principles.

> "*The implication ... is that somehow an identity is something only women or African-Americans or perhaps LGBT people have.*"

All Politics Is Identity Politics

Matthew Yglesias

In the following viewpoint, Matthew Yglesias argues that all politics is essentially identity politics—except that some people are blind to this fact because of their privilege. According to Yglesias, politics itself is defined as making "collective decisions" for the better good. This necessitates that individual identities are involved in the decision-making process. Unfortunately, certain identities are more associated with identity politics than others, making it seem, to some, like "gendered or ethnic claims" against "pure selves and neutral rationality." The truth is much more nuanced than this, according to Yglesias, and everyone, no matter their race, ethnicity, or gender, involves their identity in their politics. Yglesias is a journalist who writes about politics for Vox.

"All Politics Is Identity Politics," by Matthew Yglesias, Vox Media, Inc., June 5, 2015. Reprinted by permission.

As you read, consider the following questions:

1. Why might the popularity of identity politics be a "useful shock" to the media?
2. According to the author, which identities are emphasized in identity politics? Why?
3. Why is identity inextricably tied to politics, according to the viewpoint?

Something that I thought I noticed soon after I graduated college and moved to DC was that a lot of my female friends were *very* interested in the subject of street harassment. Later, thanks to the magic of social media and web traffic I learned that I'd misconstrued this entirely. It's not that *women I was friends with* were very interested in this subject. *Women in general* were interested. Their interest wasn't exactly invisible to me—I was hearing about it in person from friends—but ten or 12 years ago those friends' interest wasn't refracted back and validated by the larger media ecosystem the way it is today. It seemed like an idiosyncratic obsession rather than what it is: an alarmingly widespread social malady that a male-dominated media culture had kind of swept under the rug.

Another thing you see in the web traffic stats is that the American public's appetite for internecine warfare between diaspora Jewish intellectuals about what is and is not the appropriate attitude to have toward Israel is quite limited.

When you stop and think about it, this is perfectly obvious (indeed, if you're not Jewish it probably didn't even require thought). But in a world where the New York Times' columnist rotation features more Jews than women of any ethnic background, it's easy for a person (like me!) with demographic attributes very typical of the prestige media to be blind to the ways particularist identities were shaping coverage decisions.

This is, I think, the problem with [the] idea of "identity politics" as a shorthand for talking about feminism or anti-racism.

The world of navel-gazing journalism is currently enmeshed in a couple of partially overlapping conversations, about "PC culture," diversity, social justice, technological change, and shifting business models. One thread of this is the (accurate) observation that social media distribution creates new incentives for publications to be attuned to feminist and minority rights perspectives in a way that was not necessarily the case in the past. But where some see a cynical play for readership, I see an extraordinarily useful shock to a media ecosystem that's too long been myopic in its range of concerns.

The implication of this usage (which is widespread, and by no means limited to people who agree with Chait) is that somehow an identity is something only women or African-Americans or perhaps LGBT people have. White men just have ideas about politics that spring from a realm of pure reason, with concerns that are by definition universal.

You see something similar in Noam Scheiber's argument that New York City Mayor Bill de Blasio went astray by emphasizing an "identity group agenda" of police reform at the expense of a (presumably identity-free) agenda of populist economics. For starters, it is actually inevitable that a New York City mayor would end up spending more time on his police department management agenda (something that is actually under the mayor's control) than on tax policy, which is set by the State Legislature in Albany.

But beyond that, not addressing a racially discriminatory status quo in policing is itself a choice. Indeed, it's a kind of identity group appeal—to white people, whose preferred means of striking the balance between liberty and security, in many contexts, is that security should be achieved by depriving *other people* of their civil liberties.

This is where the at-times tiresome concept of privilege becomes very useful. The truth is that almost all politics is, on some level, about identity. But those with the right identities have the privilege of simply calling it politics while labeling other people's agendas "identity."

Denial of this reality, it seems to me, is actually a key failing of a certain brand of American liberalism. Conservatives may join some white male liberals in decrying "identity politics," but nobody knows better than conservatives the power and importance of identities like Christian, American, traditional family, etc., in shaping thinking and giving meaning to political engagement.

Indeed, we just saw a species of this failure of American liberalism in the Obama administration's swiftly abandoned plan to kill tax-subsidized 529 accounts. The entire politics of this ended up hinging not on economic models, but on the question of whether a certain class of professional couple earning a low-six figure income should be considered "middle class." Or look at how Obama's effort to raise middle-class incomes in a way that encourages work morphed into a "war on homemakers."

All politics is, on some level, identity politics. The idea that it's some special attribute of black politics or feminist politics is just blindness. And while identity politics can be practiced in bad ways or in pursuit of bad goals, that's simply to say that *politics* can be practiced both for good and for ill. The idea that gendered or ethnic claims are despoiling a liberalism of pure selves and neutral rationality is little more than an unselfconscious form of identity politics. Politics is about collective decisions. This necessarily implicates individuals' identities by defining who is inside and who is outside the community of concern and under what terms.

The trend by which modern digital media forces publications to be more aware of what resonates with audiences is not an unalloyed good. But given the centrality of identity to politics of all kinds and the badly skewed demographics at the commanding heights of the American media ecosystem, *this particular aspect* of the trend is pretty clearly change for the better.

> *"Demonstrating the pleasures and benefits of co-operative, compassionate organisation offers a strong threat to the world of borders and guards."*

Compassion Is More Useful Than Identity Politics

Jamie Heckert

In the following viewpoint, Jamie Heckert leverages a critique of identity politics from the progressive left. He states that identity politics misses the mark because it solidifies divides among people and, thus, stifles compassion. Simple acts of compassion, Heckert suggests, may be more useful to overturning social hierarchy and oppression than political organizing done through identity politics. Heckert uses a quote by the feminist academic Audre Lorde—"The master's tools will never dismantle the master's house"—to show how tools of division and hierarchical societies, like identity politics, will never dismantle the systems they attempt to critique. Heckert earned a PhD from the University of Edinburgh and is a founding member of Anarchist Studies Network and coeditor of Anarchism & Sexuality: Ethics, Relationships and Power.

"Maintaining the Borders: Identity & Politics," by Jamie Heckert, The Anarchist Library, October 30, 2002. Reprinted by permission.

As you read, consider the following questions:

1. How does the author distinguish identity from the beginning of the viewpoint?
2. What is one of the many reasons the author gives for why identity politics fails?
3. Why does the author say that radical politics are not appealing?

Identity is the process of creating and maintaining borders, creating different *kinds of people*. This keeps the world packaged in tidy little boxes. These boxes, in turn, are necessary for the violence and domination of hierarchical societies. There cannot be masters or slaves, bosses or workers, men or women, whites or blacks, leaders or followers, heterosexuals or queers, without identity.

Social movement[1], both past and present, often attempts to use identity as a tool of liberation. Movement based on gender, sexual orientation, class, ethnic and ability identities all have some success in challenging hierarchy and oppression. By no means do I mean to diminish the impact of past and present activism. Personally, my life would have been much more difficult before feminist and gay liberation/equality movement arose. I argue that identity politics is inherently limited in its ability to challenge hierarchy because it depends upon the same roots as the system it aims to overthrow. "The master's tools will never dismantle the master's house."[2]

Does that Mean We Should all Be the Same?

Identity is also the answer to the question, "who am I?". This is different from answering, "what *kind* of person am I?". Labels like "woman", "white" and "heterosexual" tell us about someone's position in various hierarchies. These positions, these identities, are significant to how a person thinks of themselves. But, they don't answer the question, "who am I?" Each of us is unique, both similar and different to everyone else in various ways. Working to eliminate identity in the hierarchical sense (e.g. some animals are more equal than others) isn't the same as eliminating identity in the individual sense (e.g. I'll still be Jamie). When I talk about the problems with identity, I mean the "boxes" rather than individuals.

Let me use "sexual orientation" as an example. Supposedly people can be put into three boxes, depending on whether they fancy women, men or both. While this is a popular idea, it seems to cause an awful lot of suffering. People worry a lot about their image, and try very hard to make sure that others realise "what" they are. We also worry about "what" other people are — are they like me or are they different? Some people are so unhappy and anxious about these things that they attack others, either physically or verbally. Even people who think of themselves as heterosexual can be attacked. Finally, people suffer when they desire others of the "wrong" gender, or if they worry that others think they do. One alternative is that we all try to be "equal opportunity lovers" and fancy everyone. Those who succeed could then feel superior to those whose desires are less politically correct. Another alternative is that we try to give up thinking of people (including ourselves) in terms of sexual orientation and instead recognise that everyone's sexual desires are complex and unique. This would mean being yourself rather than a heterosexual, a queer or whatever, and to recognise people as people instead of members of categories. We could never all be the same, even if we tried!

What is Wrong with Political Identity?

Identity separates people. It encourages us to believe that "we" are different from "others." Identity can also encourage conformity. How else do I show that I am *one of us* other than conforming to the accepted codes prescribed to that identity? This construction of similarity and difference exists whether we are talking about traditional identity politics groups like "disabled people" or political identities like "environmentalists." This separation of *us* from *them* has serious consequences for political movement.

Identity encourages isolation. Political ghettos cannot exist without political identity; and their existence reinforces it. Not only are the "activists" separated from the "non-activists," but within a broad political ghetto, *anarchists, feminists,* and *environmentalists* (amongst others) often see themselves as involved in separate struggles. People who consider themselves politically active are separated both from each other and from others who do not share an "activist" identity. Effective movement for radical social change cannot be based on such divisions.

Identity reduces social phenomena to individuals. Concepts like anarchism and racism are social. They are not embodied by individuals as terms like "anarchist" and "racist" suggest. Rather, they exist as ideas, practices and relationships. In most societies, racism is inherent in our institutionalised relationships and ways of thinking. We can and should be critical of racism, but to attack people as "racists" can only further alienate them from our efforts.[3] Besides, it is a dangerous fantasy to believe that "racists" can be separated from those of us who are non-racist. Likewise, anarchism exists throughout every society. Every time people co-operate without coercion to achieve shared goals, that is anarchy. Every time someone thinks that people should be able to get along with each other without domination, that is anarchism. If we only see racism in "racists," we will never effectively challenge racism. If we only see anarchism in "anarchists," we will miss out on so many desperately needed sources of inspiration.

Identity encourages purity. If we believe that concepts like feminism can be embodied in individuals, then some people can be more feminist than others. This leads to debates about "real feminists" and how feminists should act (e.g. debates regarding feminism and heterosexuality). Feminist purity allows for hierarchy (e.g. more or less and thus better or worse feminists) and encourages guilt (e.g. asking yourself "should real feminists think/act like this?").

Political identity simplifies personal identity. A related problem for feminist identity, for example, is that it demands we focus on one aspects of our complex lives. Feminist movement has often been dominated by white middle-class women who have a particular perspective on what is a "women's issue." Many women have had to choose between involvement in a woman's movement that fails to recognise ethnicity and class issues, or in black or working class politics that did not acknowledge gender. But, the alternative of specialised identity politics could get very silly (e.g. a group for disabled, transgender, lesbian, working-class women of colour). Likewise, if I describe myself as **a** feminist, **an** anarchist, and **a** sex radical, I am suddenly three different people. However, if I say I advocate feminism, anarchism and radical sexual politics I am one person with a variety of beliefs.[4]

Identity often imagines easily defined interests. Feminism is often presented as for women only; men are perceived to entirely benefit from the gender system. Many men do clearly benefit from the gender system in terms of institutionalised domination. If we perceive interests as inherently stemming from current systems, we fail to recognise how people would benefit from alternative systems. If we want to encourage and inspire people to create a very different form of society, we should share with each other what we see as beneficial. We must recognise that different value systems (e.g. domination versus compassion) result in very different interests.

Identity discourages participation. If people are worried that they might be excluded through labelling (e.g. racist or homophobic), they won't feel welcomed and won't get involved. Likewise, people do not get involved if they believe that it is not in their interests. If we perpetuate the idea that feminism is for women, men will never see how it could also be in their interests to support feminism. Or they might support feminism, but feel guilty for their male privilege. Either way, men are not encouraged to be active in feminist movements. Radical social change requires mass social movement. Identity politics, by definition, can never achieve this. Political identities, like "environmentalist", can likewise become a basis for minority politics.

Identity creates opposition. By dividing the world up into opposing pairs (e.g. men/women, heterosexuals/queers, ruling class/working-class, whites/blacks), identity creates opposite types of people who perceive themselves as having opposing interests. This opposition means that people fail to recognise their common interests as human beings. The opposition of two forces pushing against each other means that very little changes.

Identity freezes the fluid. Neither individual identity (the "who am I?" kind) nor social organisation are fixed, but are in constant motion. Political identities require that these fluid processes are frozen realities with particular characteristics and inherent interests. In failing to recognise the nature of both identity and society, political identity can only inhibit radical social change.

It May not Be Perfect, but Can't it Still Be a Useful Strategy?

It is a very good strategy if you don't want to change things very much. Identity politics fits in nicely within the dominant neo-liberal ideology. Groups created around oppressed identities can lobby the state for civil rights. This idea of trying to protect individuals without changing relationships or systems of organisation is compatible with the individualistic basis of capitalism and representative "democracy."

I would never argue that a strategy has to be "perfect" to be useful, but it must be consistent with its aims. Ends and means can only be separated in our minds. If the aim is to reduce or eliminate hierarchical social divisions (e.g. gender, ethnicity, nationality, sexual orientation, class), a strategy which depends upon those very divisions can never be successful.

If Political Identity Is Such a Poor Strategy, Why Is it So Common?

On a personal level, political identity makes us feel part of something larger at the same time that it makes us feel special were different. In the short-term, this can be very successful defence mechanism. For example, I'm sure I would have been a lot more damaged by the sexist and homophobic environment in which I grew up if I had not been able to convert stigma into pride. However, feeling yourself to be different and separate from other people is not a successful long-term strategy, either psychologically or politically.

What's the Alternative to Political Identity?

If borders are the problem, then we must support and encourage each other to tear down the fences. Two crucial tools for dismantling borders are systematic analyses and compassionate strategies.

We should recognise oppression is not simply a practice of individuals who have power over those who do not. Instead, we could see how forms of organisation (including institutions and relationships) *systematically* produce hierarchies and borders. People will only see an interest in getting more involved if they realise that their individual problems—anxiety, depression, exhaustion, anger, poverty, meaningless work, unsatisfying sex lives, etc—are not unique, but are systematically produced. Furthermore, their action will only be effective if they work to reduce all forms of hierarchy and domination. Constructs including gender, sexuality, capitalism, race and the nation state are interdependent systems. Each system of domination serves to reinforce the others. This doesn't mean we have to solve every problem instantly, but we must recognise that all issues are human issues. At the same time, we must not imagine that a particular system of domination (not even capitalism!) is the source of all others.

Radical politics is rarely appealing because it focuses on the evils of the world. This offers little that is hopeful or constructive in people's daily lives. If we want to see widespread social movement for radical change, we have to offer people something *they* value. Listening to people's concerns, caring about their problems and encouraging and supporting them to develop systemic solutions requires compassion. Offer people a better quality of life instead of focusing so much on depressing aspects of our current society.

We should also recognise that people positioned in more privileged categories may in some ways suffer. At the very least, people who feel a strong need to dominate and control must suffer deep insecurities, the results of competition and hierarchy. Insecurity, domination and control are not conducive to fulfilling and meaningful relationships with other people. Attacking people in "privileged" positions does little to dismantle these systems. It also gives entirely too much credit to people in those positions —they are both products and producers of systems, just like the rest of us.

To radically reorganise our society, we should aim to both diminish systematic domination and suffering and encourage systematic compassion. Just as apparently disconnected and often incoherent forms of domination can reinforce and maintaining each other, so too can a compassionate organisation of society become systematic and self-sustaining.

Encouraging people to be more comfortable with sexuality in general has been a key focus of my own political efforts. But, sexuality is only one area in which a compassionate and systematic approach has much more radical potential than politicising identity.

Find sources of suffering, whatever they are, and support and encourage people to find ways of relating to themselves and others that reduce that suffering. Help build compassionate, co-operative institutions (e.g. social centres, support/discussion groups, mediation services, childcare support, food not bombs). Tell people when you admire or appreciate their efforts. Support people trying to change their environments (e.g. workplace resistance). Offer alternatives to people who are involved in or considering authoritarian positions (e.g. military, police, business management).

Demonstrating the pleasures and benefits of co-operative, compassionate organisation offers a strong threat to the world of borders and guards. I suspect that fragmented groups, anti-whatever demonstrations, unfriendly, exclusive meetings and utopian "after the revolution" lectures will never be quite as enticing to people outside the activist ghetto.

Notes

1. Following bell hooks, I refer to social movement, rather than maintaining that boundaries can be placed around identifiable "social movements."

2. See Audre Lorde, "The Master's Tools Will Never Dismantle the Master's House," pp110-112 in *Sister Out-sider: Essays and Speeches* (1984), who took the title from an old US civil rights adage.

3. See Border Camps : The New "Sexy" Thing? in this issue.

4. See pretty much anything by bell hooks for more on this.

> *"Identity politics thus is zero-sum:
> what helps one group is thought
> inevitably to harm another; what
> benefits them must hurt me. It is a
> politics of despair."*

Identity Politics Has Become a Zero-Sum Game

Joan D. Mandle

In the following viewpoint, author Joan D. Mandle examines how identity politics emerged during second-wave feminism and the women's liberation movement. While she stresses the victories of "women's lib," she also acknowledges that the form of identity politics that has emerged has, ultimately, become harmful to contemporary feminism. For Mandle, contemporary identity politics is a "zero-sum" game where it is believed that one group can prosper only if another group suffers. For feminism to have a future, she states, contemporary feminists must separate themselves from identity politics (and, thus, "difference feminism" and "victim feminism") and organize across a broader range of alliances. Mandle is associate professor of sociology at Colgate University.

As you read, consider the following questions:

1. What do you think the women's liberation movement slogan "the personal is political" means? How does it relate to identity politics?
2. According to Mandle, what was the background out of which identity politics grew?
3. Why does Mandel call identity politics a "zero-sum" game?

Second Wave Feminism

One of the best known and most important political slogans of the early Women's Liberation Movement in which I was involved in the middle 1960s claimed that "the personal is political." That phrase was honed in reaction to struggles within the 1960s social movements out of which the Women's Liberation Movement first emerged. It captured the insight that many of what were thought to be personal problems possessed social and political causes, were widely shared among women, and could only be resolved by social and political change.

In the 1960s social movements—the Civil Rights Movement, the movement against the War in Vietnam, and the student movement which called for more student rights and decision-making power on college campuses—women were central actors. Within all these movements, however, women activists were denied the recognition and the responsibility that they deserved and that they had earned. Despite their commitment and contributions, they were all too often refused leadership positions, treated as second class citizens, told to make coffee, and put on display as sex objects. By the middle 1960s many of these women began to react to and organize around the strong contradiction within social movements which fought for self-determination and equality and yet which denied these same basic rights within their own ranks. First in the civil rights movement, with a statement written by Mary King and Casey Hayden, and soon afterward and more frequently in the anti-war movement, SDS, and other social movements, women radicals began to demand equity and respect as activists.

The reaction of many of their male and female comrades seems predictable in retrospect, but was shocking and demoralizing at the time. Women's claims were met with derision, ridicule, and the political argument that they were worrying about "personal" issues and in this way draining movement effectiveness in fighting the "political" injustices of racism and imperialism. How could women be so selfish, it was asked, to focus on their personal disgruntlement when black people were denied voting privileges in Mississippi, peasants were being napalmed in Vietnam, and students were treated as numbers in large faceless bureaucratic universities?

Movement women had no shortage of responses to these objections, but the one that became a mantra of the new women's movement emerging out of these struggles was the claim that personal lives—relationships with friends, lovers, political comrades —were not personal at all but characterized by power and fraught with political meaning. Women argued that assumptions that they were followers and men leaders, that women naturally were "better" with children and men "better" at organizing, that women should type and men should discuss issues—that all these assumptions were deeply political, denying women not only equality within progressive movements, but even more basically the freedom to choose for themselves what they could and should think and do. When most men and some of the women involved within the 60s movements refused to listen, many women left the movement to, as they put it at the time, "organize around our own oppression." They began a liberation movement dedicated to eliminating the ways in which women were constrained and harmed by sexist assumptions and behavior.

By and large the early women's movement, emerging from a political critique of what was defined as "personal" both in progressive movements and in the wider society, pressed for the removal of the social barriers and obstacles that had constrained women's choices. This was true with respect to a wide range of issues including reproductive choice, educational and occupational options, legal rights, as well as sexual orientation and personal relationships. The movement was intent on achieving social justice which it defined as providing women and men with similar opportunities to grow, develop, express, and exercise their potential as people. The political analysis underlying this vision of personal fulfillment asserted that elimination of the sexism which pervaded political and social institutional arrangements and attitudes was the best way of ensuring that every one, regardless of sex, would have the ability to exercise personal freedom.

Successes were many during those early years. The decades of the 60s and 70s were in fact characterized by enormous change in the range of behavior and choices open to women in our society. Consciousness was raised, and attitudes of both men and women underwent significant change concerning women's capabilities and rights, while the notion of equality between the sexes gained increased legitimacy. Change was especially rapid in the law during those years. Indeed, Jane Mansbridge notes that had the ERA [Equal Rights Amendment] been passed in 1982, its effect would have been largely symbolic because almost all sex-differentiated (sexist) laws which such an amendment would have changed had already been altered by that time.

The social and political changes effected by the early women's movement thus were in the service of a sex-neutral model of society. In this, each individual would be afforded an equal opportunity to shape her or his own life regardless of sex. The notion of gender difference was deemphasized by a movement focused on equality, as women sought to gain the right to fully participate in all aspects of society. Differences between women and men, which had consistently been a central ideological and behavioral component of limiting women to a separate stereotyped "feminine" sphere, came under attack. The personal fact of one's sex became an arena of political struggle, as increasing numbers of feminists challenged the prevailing ideology that sex and gender were legitimate constraints on the right to self-determination. Political justice demanded that gender make no difference. Expectations were high that women would achieve the freedom they had been denied and that sexism would be defeated.

But in the 1980s much of this changed. The country as a whole became more conservative in all areas of political life, as the Right, with Ronald Reagan as its standard bearer, launched what Susan Faludi has referred to as a "Blacklash" against the progressive changes of the previous decades. As the gains of the women's movement began to slow, many feminists became discouraged with the continuation of sexist attitudes and behavior. The gap between incomes for women and men narrowed but remained stubbornly persistent, abortion rights came under renewed attack, and awareness of and concern about the extent of harassment and violence against women increased. This latter ironically reflected the Women's Movement's earlier success, for due to its efforts behavior previously regarded as legally unproblematic, such as sexual harassment at work or marital and date rape, was criminalized, and increased reporting of violence occurred. In addition, growing numbers of women found themselves doing what Arlie Hochschild has called the "Second Shift"—working at full time jobs during the day and a second job at home as they continued to assume most or all of the burden of home and child care in their families. Finally, even though the 1970s were the heyday of the Movement, increasing numbers of young girls at that time were being raised in poverty because their single mothers' former husbands or lovers contributed nothing to support them, were becoming painfully aware of the dangers of abuse, rape, and sexual harassment, and were discouraged by their mothers struggles with the double burden of work and family care. As these girls matured into young women in the 1980s, many were far from convinced that the women's movement had liberated anybody. All of these problems affecting women seemed to fly in the face of feminism's promises and expectations of equality, and some women, discouraged with the pace of change and the persistence of sexism, reacted by retreating from claims for equality and from demands for social change.

But as the 1980s progressed, it was not only feminists who were experiencing disillusionment and increasing pessimism. In an era when the conservative politics of Reaganism were dominant, the tragedy was that no compelling alternative progressive world-view was being constructed. A vision of a society of fairness and justice was not offered to counter the conservative hegemony, and the attainment of an egalitarian society seemed less and less possible.

Identity Politics

Out of this situation there emerged what has been called identity politics, a politics that stresses strong collective group identities as the basis of political analysis and action. As political engagement with the society as a whole was increasingly perceived to have produced insufficient progress or solutions, and in the absence of a compelling model of a society worth struggling for, many progressives retreated into a focus on their own "self" and into specific cultural and ideological identity groups which made rights, status, and privilege claims on the basis of a victimized identity. These groups included ethnic minorities such as African-Americans, Asian-Americans, Native Americans, religious groups, lesbian women and gay men, deaf and other disabled people. The desire to gain sympathy on the basis of a tarnished identity was sometimes taken to absurd lengths, as for example when privileged white men pronounced themselves victims based on their alleged oppression by women and especially by feminists. Indeed in the last decade there has been an explosion of groups vying with one another for social recognition of their oppression and respect for it. This has been especially exaggerated on college campuses where young people have divided into any number of separate identity groups.

Identity politics is centered on the idea that activism involves groups' turning inward and stressing separatism, strong collective identities, and political goals focused on psychological and personal self-esteem. Jeffrey Escofier, writing about the gay movement, defines identity politics in the following fashion:

> The politics of identity is a kind of cultural politics. It relies on the development of a culture that is able to create new and affirmative conceptions of the self, to articulate collective identities, and to forge a sense of group loyalty. Identity politics—very much like nationalism—requires the development of rigid definitions of the boundaries between those who have particular collective identities and those who do not.

Many progressive activists today have come to base their political analysis on collectively and often ideologically constructed identities which are seen as immutable and all-encompassing. These identities, for many, provide a retreat where they can feel "comfortable" and "safe" from the assaults and insults of the rest of the society. Today it is the case that many of those who profess a radical critique of society nonetheless do not feel able, as activists in the 60s and 70s did, to engage people outside their own self-defined group—either to press for improvement in their disadvantaged status or to join in coalition. Identity politics defines groups as so different from one another, with the gap dividing them so wide and unbridgeable, that interaction is purposeless. Not only is it assumed that working together will inevitably fail to bring progressive change that would benefit any particular group. In addition, identity groups discourage political contact because of their concern that the psychological injury and personal discomfort they believe such contact inevitably entails will harm individuals' self-esteem and erode their identity.

Identity politics thus is zero-sum: what helps one group is thought inevitably to harm another; what benefits them must hurt me. It is a politics of despair. In the name of advancing the interests of one's own group, it rejects attempts to educate, pressure, or change the society as a whole, thus accepting the status quo and revealing its essentially conservative nature. Identity politics advocates a retreat into the protection of the self based on the celebration of group identity. It is a politics of defeat and demoralization, of pessimism and selfishness. By seizing as much as possible for one's self and group, it exposes its complete disregard for the whole from which it has separated—for the rest of the society. Identity politics thus rejects the search for a just and comprehensive solution to social problems.

Feminism and Identity Politics

Like other progressive social movements, feminism has been deeply affected by the growth of identity politics. Within feminism, identity politics has taken two often-related forms which, together, I believe to be hegemonic today. One is generally referred to as difference or essentialist feminism, and the other as victim feminism. Difference feminism emphasizes the unique identity of women as a group, stressing and usually celebrating essential female characteristics which it believes make women different from—indeed even opposite to—men. Victim feminism also assumes that women have a unique identity, but the focus of that identity is women's victimization on the basis of sex, typically at the hands of men.

In defining difference feminism, Wendy Kaminer has stated that, by suggesting that women differ from men in a myriad of ways, it identifies "feminism with femininity." In what is perhaps the most influential version of this ideology, popularized in the work of Carol Gilligan, difference feminism emphasizes that women share "a different voice, different moral sensibilities—an ethic of care." According to Kaminer, this notion of female difference is attractive to feminists and non-feminists alike for a number of reasons. Difference feminism appeals to some feminists, she asserts, because it revalues previously devalued characteristics such as emotionality and social connectedness which women are thought to embody. In declaring female traits superior to those such as aggression and rationality which characterize men, difference feminism seems to reject sexism by turning it on its head. It thus provides a clear group identity for women which stresses the way they are special.

According to Kaminer, difference feminism is also attractive to feminists in another manner. She argues that it allows feminists to be angry at men and challenge their hegemony without worrying that they are giving up their femininity. Because they are socialized to fear the loss of femininity, the advocacy of radical change in gender roles is deeply threatening to many women, including feminists. Difference feminism's reassertion of the value of femininity helps to assuage these fears and thus seems to make feminism more acceptable. Finally, even some non-feminists are drawn to difference feminism because it legitimates a belief in immutable and natural sex differences, a central tenet of conservative claims for support of the status quo. As noted above, this conservative bias is a pivotal element of difference feminism.

What Naomi Wolf has called victim feminism also reinforces identity politics, for victim feminism also assumes women's diametrical difference from men as a central component of its view. According to victim feminism, however, what is unique about women's difference is that they are powerless to affect the victim status by which they are primarily defined. Wolf argues that victim feminism "turns suffering and persecution into a kind of glamour." The attractiveness of this model is partially due to the fact that feminists understand all too well the discouraging reality that women have been and continue to be victims of sexism, male violence, and discrimination. But victim feminism is attractive to others primarily because it absolves individuals of the political responsibility to act to change their own condition. Its emphasis on personal victimization includes a refusal to hold women in any way responsible for their problems. It thus implies that, as a group, women are helpless in the face of the overwhelming factors which force them to accept—however unhappily—the circumstances in which they find themselves.

Such a view of women resonates with many non-feminists as well because it pictures women as passive and in need of protection, a view consistent with traditionally sexist ideas of women and femininity. And finally, victim feminism is popular because it is consistent with the explosion of self-help programs and talk shows where individuals—disproportionately women—compete for public recognition of their claims to personally victimized status. These shows try—all too successfully—to convince their audiences and even perhaps their guests that exposing personal problems on television is itself a solution to them, in this way delegitimating the serious political changes which many such problems require for their elimination.

The hegemony of identity politics within feminism, in my view, has helped to stymie the growth of a large scale feminist movement which could effectively challenge sexism and create the possibility of justice and fairness in our society. On the one hand identity politics makes the coalitions needed to build a mass movement for social change extremely difficult. With its emphasis on internal group solidarity and personal self-esteem, identity politics divides potential allies from one another. Difference feminism makes the task for example of including men in the struggle against sexism almost impossible, and even trying to change men's behavior or attitudes is made to seem futile because of the assumption that the sexes share so little. Indeed some difference feminists assert that women and men are so different from one another that they can hardly communicate across sex at all. The phrase "Men don't get it" too often implies that they "can't" get it, because, it is argued by difference feminists, only women have the capacity to really understand what other women are talking about. This of course is nonsense without any empirical validity, but identity politics so strongly stresses sex differences that this has come to be the accepted wisdom.

But it is not just coalitions across sex that are assumed to be impossible, but coalitions among women as well. One of the problems with identity politics is that its assumptions can lead to an almost infinite number of smaller and smaller female identity groups. Identity politics puts a premium on valuing and exaggerating differences existing among women as well as those that are cross-sex. This makes large and potentially powerful feminist organizations difficult to sustain. One example of this effect was the problem of fractionalization within the National Women's Studies Association (NWSA) some years ago, largely due to the many splits that occurred within its ranks. Identity groups organized within the organization pitting academic women against non-academic, Jewish women against non-Jews, women of color against white women, lesbians against straight women, lesbians of color against white lesbians, mothers against non-mothers and more. Each group focused on its own identity, its own victimization which it set up in competition with others' claims of victim status, and ins response to which it demanded recognition and concessions from the organization. The center—if it existed—simply could not hold and the organization, which had played a very important role in creating and supporting women's studies programs on campuses, was wracked by years of conflict from which it has only recently recovered.

Thus, by stressing the characteristics which divide us, the logic of identity politics is that ultimately each individual is her own group. If each individual is different from all others, then to protect herself adequately she needs to be selfish—to ally with no one and to count only on herself to protect her interests. It is obvious that this stance makes it completely impossible to bring together the large numbers of people necessary successfully to press for social change. Coalitions fail to develop or are not even attempted. In this way, identity politics within feminism, as elsewhere, is basically conservative, working against progressive change and supporting the status quo.

The divisions promoted by identity politics are especially pronounced today on college campuses. Not only between male and female students but also among students of different racial and ethnic backgrounds, differences are perceived as unbridgeable barriers and victimized status is a badge of honor. It is especially ironic that this separation is occurring at precisely the moment in history when real differences among students are less pronounced than ever in the past. American society is in fact culturally very homogeneous, as almost all young Americans who attend college grow up watching the same television programs, shopping at the same malls, listening to the same music, and eating the same fast food for large portions of their lives. Beginning salaries for students who graduate from elite universities have increasingly become similar by race and sex. But the identity politics which is hegemonic on such elite college campuses emphasizes difference above all else, even when students have trouble actually articulating what, in concrete terms, those significant differences are.

The focus of attention within the context of identity politics becomes building solidarity and loyalty within one's own group. The outcome divides students from one another. Female students of different ethnic groups, for example, come to see themselves as having nothing in common with one another, and to compete over their relative degree of victimization. Feminist women of color, for example, on many campuses including Colgate's separate from white feminists, and take as a major task the goal of criticizing and creating guilt in white women students for their alleged racist attitudes. Similarly, within groups of women of color the same process occurs, with different ethnic groups dividing off and emphasizing the large differences among them. On other campuses, it is lesbian women who claim an especially oppressed status and, stressing their differences from straight women, critique the attitudes and behavior of heterosexual women towards them. Regardless of the merit of any particular critique, this model of identity politics effectively divides from one another those who could be allies in facing the many real problems—of poverty, violence, reproductive control, and work/ family conflict—that women share when facing the world outside the university. Though in fact female college students share large numbers of issues around which they could build an inclusive movement to attack sexist behavior and attitudes, they turn inward, reinforcing their own feelings of victimization and loyalty, and typically turn outward only to attack one another.

In addition to dividing potential allies from one another, identity politics' dominance of feminism creates other obstacles to effective struggles for social change. Its focus on personal identity produces a kind of a-political narcissism. Its attempt is to redefine politics as the attempt to know and assert "who I am" as part of a specifically narrow group. The notion that politics should involve responsibility toward others as well as toward oneself and toward whatever one defines as one's "own group" has been lost. The assertion of one's selfhood, concern with one's own self-esteem, as well as group loyalty become ends, the primary goals of political expression. In addition to its inward-looking focus, the strong emphasis on group loyalty characteristic of identity politics creates exaggerated emotional dependence on the group and consequently enormous pressure towards conformity and away from dissenting or independent thought. Stephen Carter, in his Confessions of An Affirmative Action Baby, exposes the damage done to independent and creative individual thinking that such a situation produces, again especially on college campuses. This exaggerated loyalty, then, also serves as an obstacle to the creation of an inclusive and thoughtful feminist politics.

The Future of Feminism

So where do we go from here? It is no doubt clear from my presentation today that my own politics are in strong contrast to identity politics. For a successful progressive politics to emerge again in our society, I believe that we need to create a political atmosphere where the zero-sum model of group competition gives way to coalitions among progressive groups to work on specific social problems; where personal issues of identity and self-esteem do not stymie individuals and groups' abilities to act politically; and where a unifying vision of fairness and social justice replaces the pessimistic focus on difference.

For those of you who agree with me, we have a difficult but important task in front of us. Difficult especially now as we see in so many parts of the world from Kosovo to Rwanda the strength of identity politics in the form of nationalism—whether organized on religious, or cultural, or regional grounds—as a rallying cry for the most inhumane acts of violence among neighbors. Our task, then, does seem to run counter to a deep-seated tendency for human beings to react with fear and even hatred to differences, whether those differences are real, socially created, or imagined. For those of you who believe as I do, our task is to convince individuals and groups mired in the search for and affirmation of difference and victimization that it is in their interests to alter the sources of their victimization by joining with others to create a just society for all. This is not to say that individual or group conflicts will or can completely disappear. There are legitimate conflicts of interest in any society. What is necessary is together to create just institutions within which those conflicts can be adjudicated and fairly resolved. Indeed we must recognize that the only possible solution to the legitimate problems and conflicts groups face is such a broad movement for social justice.

For feminism, these issues presently constitute a crisis of definition, as well as a choice about how to proceed. In *Fire With Fire*, Naomi Wolf offers a number of different definitions of feminism. Two however seem particularly instructive in the present context. In one portion of the book she advocates a definition of feminism that focuses on difference, on "more for women," including anything as feminist that "makes women stronger in ways that each woman is entitled to define for herself" and allowing that a woman is a feminist if she "respects herself" and is "operating at her full speed." This identity and difference-oriented definition is one direction in which feminism may continue to go. Feminists in this view would include Phyllis Schlafly and Margaret Thatcher for surely they respect themselves and believe they have defined ways to make women stronger. This brand of feminism would focus on getting more for women regardless of the implication for others and would advocate the use of their newly attained power for good or evil, as they individually decide. For reasons outlined in this paper, I reject this view.

In the same book, however, Wolf proposes another definition of feminism. Here she emphasizes feminism's essence as a movement for a socially more just society. This then is the other possible direction that feminism today could take, reaching out to others who share a commitment to a just and egalitarian society and building the coalitions necessary to exercise the power to move in that direction. Concrete examples of such possibilities abound. Poor women, especially the young who cannot afford abortions, could join with middle class pro-choice advocates in pressing for the federal funding necessary if all women are to have real reproductive control. The crisis in day care—both its inadequate availability and quality—has the potential to unite working parents of all ethnicities and social classes. Issues such as rape, battering, and sexual harassment cut across class and race and age, pointing the way to broad-based coalitions of women and men who are outraged by these crimes. And the continued low-pay, dead end, and sex stereotyped jobs in which women find themselves could be addressed as part of the broader fight for better education and higher paying jobs in the American economy as a whole, as feminists join with unions and other advocates of higher incomes for working people.

These and other issues have the potential of combining the political influence of disparate groups which can agree on specific issues and are willing to work together to effect concrete change in the functioning of our laws and institutions. As we look to our future, we also need to be cognizant of our past. In the early 1960s when the Second Wave of feminism began, the women's movement was separate, but at the same time part of a larger number of groups —Civil Rights, anti-war, New Left, student groups—committed to and optimistic about constructing a more just society for all. These earliest feminists understood that women's personal problems had social origins and that they thus required political solutions, necessarily involving the entire society. If today we focus only on ourselves, our differences, and on our own victimization, we risk repeating the mistake made by feminism in the later 1960s and early 1970s. At that time, some feminist activists began using small consciousness raising groups in a therapeutic fashion, as a way of focusing primarily on their own personal problems. Discouraged about the extent of sexism they had uncovered and demoralized by seeing themselves as its victims, they turned inward, preoccupied with the personally damaging effects of sexism. They abandoned consciousness raising groups as a way of linking themselves with others, as a way of connecting personal issues to political activism in the wider society. Isolated from larger struggles for social justice, most consciousness raising groups collapsed within a very short number of years.

Today's identity politics, both in the form of difference and victim feminism, poses a similar danger to a successful struggle to overcome sexism. The personal in these contexts is not political, primarily because it involves separation from political engagement with others in society. Rather it accepts the pessimistic—ultimately conservative—view that victimization is not amenable to change through political struggle. It accepts the notion that difference between women and men makes coalition impossible and sexism inevitable. In contrast, we need to affirm the early women's movements' insight that the personal—sexism in personal relationships, the tragedy of sexual violence or abuse, the division of housework within families, or the poverty that women disproportionately experience—can be an important factor in creating a politics of engagement. By so doing, we can join with others to construct a vision and politics that promises real democratic participation, self-determination, and egalitarian justice for all.

> "A new political order is being
> forged in front of our very eyes, and
> authoritarian white populists are
> swinging the hammer."

White Nationalism Is a Powerful Political Force

Ned Resnikoff

In the following viewpoint, Ned Resnikoff examines the political history of white nationalism up through the present day. According to Resnikoff, white nationalism has succeeded in drawing in an alarming number of voters from both the political left and the center because of its flexibility, particularly in revamping the inflammatory language it uses. As the political center is losing its footing in increasingly divisive times—both in the United States and in Europe—white nationalism is gaining more political power and bringing more people over to its side. This is one worrisome effect of organizing based on identity politics today, argues the author. Resnikoff is a journalist who has reported and written for ThinkProgress, IBT Media, Al Jazeera America, and msnbc.com.

"The Center Has Fallen, and White Nationalism Is Filling the Vacuum," by Ned Resnikoff, ThinkProgress, January 5, 2017. Reprinted by permission.

As you read, consider the following questions:

1. What was the so-called Third Way in the Clinton Era?
2. Why might white nationalism's "flexibility" make the movement more dangerous?
3. How does the author suggest white nationalists are beginning to take on power at the state level?

In 1992, a magnetic young Democrat swept aside twelve years of unbroken Republican rule by campaigning on a platform that seemed to cross the old left-right divide. Arkansas governor Bill Clinton, the first Democratic president elected after the Cold War, was the great prophet of the Third Way, a seemingly post-ideological marriage of "pro-growth" economic thinking and moderate social liberalism.

It was an idea whose time had come; with the dust still clearing from the collapse of the Berlin Wall, both market liberalism and political liberalism appeared to have vanquished their final great enemy. And in the 24 years since the end of the Civil Rights era, Baby Boomers had spawned an entirely new generation of voters—one that had never known life under Jim Crow. Third Way adherents branded themselves as heralds of a new political order, to replace the interminable squabbling between left and right that had marked prior generations. The same year that Clinton won the presidency, that view received some prestigious intellectual corroboration thanks to the publication of political theorist Francis Fukuyama's *The End of History and the Last Man,* a book that posited the world had reached "the end point of mankind's ideological evolution and the universalization of Western liberal democracy as the final form of human government."

But then another 24 years went by. Today, history has returned with a vengeance. The Third Way legacy is in tatters.

America's next president will not be a centrist, managerial liberal in the Clinton mold. Instead it will be Donald Trump, an authoritarian demagogue who is in thrall to a league of white nationalists. Even before he won the 2016 presidential election, Trump was chipping away at bedrock democratic safeguards by flirting with political violence, casting doubt on the legitimacy of democratic institutions, and undermining the electorate's perception of reality itself. "The final form of human government" is now in grave danger.

Trump has also destroyed crucial elements of Third Way's economic agenda. His candidacy signaled the end of any bipartisan support for neoliberal trade deals. And instead of taking a technocratic, managerial approach to economic policy, he has personalized it. In the weeks between his election victory and his inauguration, he has struck backroom deals with individual manufacturers and investors in order to keep jobs in the United States—or, at least, in order to look like he's keeping jobs in the United States.

The collapse of the Third Way project is not confined to the United States. The European Union, as both a liberal internationalist project and an experiment in continental free trade, is bleeding out from a thousand cuts. Last year, the United Kingdom voters narrowly approved a referendum to leave the EU, and Italy may soon do the same. Trumpian right-wing nationalists have become serious electoral contenders in France, Germany, the Netherlands, and elsewhere. They lost the most recent Austrian election by only a slim margin. In Sweden, they hold the balance of power in parliament, and in a handful of former Eastern Bloc states—most notably Hungary—they control the government.

A new political order is being forged in front of our very eyes, and authoritarian white populists are swinging the hammer. The leaders of this movement want nothing less than ideological hegemony across the entire West—an end to history, of sorts, but not anything like what Fukuyama had in mind. Even if they fall short of that lofty goal, they will have nonetheless reshaped Western politics for at least a generation.

White populism is unequivocally a movement of the right. But it is not strictly limited by the ideological and electoral constraints that often bind right-wing political movements. This is one of its great strengths; it is why white populists have managed to capture both voters and intellectuals who nominally reside on the left. Instead of pulling those new recruits toward an imaginary center, it is drawing them into radical white nationalism, and changing the nature of both left and right politics in the process.

And so Western democracy faces the greatest threat to its existence in at least a generation. This is a different kind of Third Way.

The Dark Twin of Clintonism

Unlike the Republican Freedom Caucus or the British Conservative Party, white populists are not beholden to right-wing economic dogma. Their flexibility is what makes them so dangerous.

Take the UK's major white nationalist party, UKIP. Whereas the ruling Conservative Party has spent the last few years slashing away at the UK's single-payer health care system, UKIP has positioned itself as a partial defender of the country's welfare state. While campaigning for the "Brexit" referendum earlier this year, UKIP leaders claimed that departure from the European Union would mean an additional £350 million per week could be spent propping up the National Health Service, UK's public sector health provider. This was a lie, but it enabled the party to position itself as a defender of both the social safety net and traditional British (mainly English) culture.

Germany's AfD, Sweden's SD, and Marine Le Pen's National Front have all adopted a similar frame. All these parties adhere to a doctrine sometimes called "welfare chauvinism," meaning they support welfare policies that benefit native-born citizens and virtually no one else. The primary force motivating these parties is ethno-nationalism, not any particular economic theory. Economic policy is "secondary, and will be sacrificed if it can bring better socio-cultural policies," Cas Mudde, an expert in right-wing populism at the University of Georgia, told ThinkProgress.

"The populist radical right, as I call them, are fairly centrist in socioeconomic terms, and a party like the National Front is strongly anti-globalization," said Mudde. "Some see them as socioeconomically center-left and socio-culturally far-right. I think that is a bit deceiving, as socio-economic issues are secondary to them, and they often vote more right-wing in parliament."

The same applies to Trump. White populism is at the core of his governing philosophy, just as it was at the core of his campaign message. While there is plenty in the Trump administration's economic agenda that should appeal to the GOP's hardline *Atlas Shrugged* fans, the president-elect seems largely disinterested in the subtleties of tax policy and funding structures. His marquee policy item is a ban on Muslim immigration.

Trump's biggest deviation from Republican economic orthodoxy is on the subject of trade. But it wouldn't be accurate to say he's "to the left" of his party when it comes to free trade agreements like NAFTA. Rather, he has adapted a form of market nationalism that is of a piece with white populism, much like the philosophy behind Brexit. Similarly, Trump's claim that he will "save" Medicare and Social Security can be considered an expression of welfare chauvinism. (Incidentally, he has not promised to save the food stamp program; approximately 40 percent of food stamp recipients are white, compared to 76 percent of Medicare beneficiaries.)

It would be tempting to argue that Trump's full-on embrace of white identity politics makes him an aberration among Republican officials. But it's more likely that he is leading the party toward a destination it was already headed for.

That's the view of political scientist Lee Drutman, a senior fellow at New America. In an August piece for Vox, Drutman described Trump's ascension as "the logical culmination of Republicans' 50-year 'Southern strategy' to make politics primarily about race and identity instead of economics."

According to Drutman, Republicans and Democrats have been "swapping" voters for decades, as the party of Richard Nixon mobilized white racial resentment to convert Southern

Democrats. In this telling, Clintonism, not Trumpism, is the aberration; Bill Clinton was only able to cobble together his center-left coalition because Republicans had not yet fully conquered the Southern white vote. By speaking the language of Southern whiteness while deftly holding together a multi-racial coalition, he exploited a window of opportunity that is now closed to Democrats.

But the key feature of Third Way politics was its economic philosophy, not Clinton's split-the-difference approach to white identity. With socialism apparently consigned to the past, Third Way proponents held up global market liberalism as the economic order of the future. The role of states was not to plan out national economies, but to tinker around the margins so that international free markets could distribute prosperity with maximum efficiency. After all, markets are more rational than political ideologies, and consumers behave more rationally than political fanatics.

Even critics of neoliberalism to its left and right tended to accept the premise that it was headed toward worldwide hegemony. But the consensus in favor of international trade and metastatic markets was always far more fragile than widely believed. Elite consensus, not popular acclamation, undergirded neoliberal policies. Voters were happy to go along with the experiment provided they saw some tangible (albeit unevenly distributed) material benefits, but few of them felt any strong commitment to the principles of market liberalism as a normative end. When it comes to economic abstractions like free trade, public opinion is elastic.

Racial attitudes are far more durable. Though race is no less a social construct than the free market, its impact on daily life is easier to trace. The experience of segregation or integration speaks to an ancient, tribal section of the human brain in a fashion that is both immediate and visceral. Psychological studies have found that many people unconsciously associate phenomena like changing neighborhood demographics with death; a rate hike by the Federal Reserve is unlikely to provoke an equivalent reaction in most Americans.

Clintonian centrism relied on elite consensus and consumer complacency; Trumpism speaks directly to white identity and white fear. It scorns anything like a coherent economic agenda, dwelling instead on the issues likeliest to provoke a visceral response among white voters. In that sense, Trumpism is the dark twin of Clintonism. Whereas Third Way apostles shed left-wing pieties so they could become technocratic stewards of the market, Trump has abandoned right-wing market orthodoxy in order to become a more effective tribune for white populism.

The Third Way consensus was relatively stable so long as it guaranteed financial stability and rising living standards. But the first sign of trouble—a recession, for instance—could open a door for its dark twin. Social dislocation, rapid demographic changes, a decline in the life expectancy of white women, and the election of America's first black president added spark and fuel to what CNN contributor Van Jones has accurately termed a "whitelash."

Steve Bannon, Donald Trump's chief strategist, saw this coming. During a 2014 talk at the Vatican, hosted by the right-wing Human Dignity Institute, Bannon predicted a worldwide "center-right revolt" partially composed of parties like UKIP and the National Front—as well as media outlets such as Breitbart, of which Bannon was CEO at the time.

"The central thing that binds [the revolt] all together is a center-right populist movement of really the middle class, the working men and women in the world who are just tired of being dictated to by what we call the party of Davos," said Bannon, referring to the Swiss town where the World Economic Forum holds annual gatherings. "A group of … people in New York that feel closer to people in London and in Berlin than they do to people in Kansas and in Colorado, and they have more of this elite mentality that they're going to dictate to everybody how the world's going to be run."

Bannon was correct about nearly everything except the "center-right" designation. Shedding the free market evangelism of the Thatcher and Reagan coalitions did not bring right-wing populism closer to the center. Instead, it drew additional voters to the radical fringes of white nationalism.

The Third Position

Last May, Mother Jones reported that the Trump campaign had chosen "one of the country's most prominent white nationalists" to be a delegate at the 2016 Republican National Convention. The campaign later attributed the selection to a "database error" and dropped the white nationalist leader, William Johnson, from its list of California delegates. But Johnson's ouster apparently didn't leave him with any hard feelings, since he went on to fund pro-Trump ads through his American National Super PAC.

Johnson was steadfast in his support for Trump throughout the 2016 presidential election, even though he was the chairperson of the American Freedom Party (AFP), a white supremacist third party that initially had a candidate of its own. The candidate, Bob Whitaker, resigned in April after months of internal bickering, freeing AFP to throw itself fully behind Trump.

Around this time, William Johnson and other party leadership also agreed to dial down its rhetoric a notch or two, the better to make white supremacy palatable to more moderate white voters. In the official AFP talking points, "white nationalists" became "white advocates," and "white genocide" became "white dispossession," according to leaked emails.

The maneuver paid off for AFP, which rightly saw Trump's campaign as the best vehicle for pushing extreme, racist ideology back into the political mainstream. And the party's evolving terminology, rather than amounting to a retreat, flowed organically from its founding ideals. Since its start in 2009, AFP has espoused a particular strain of white supremacism known as Third Position ideology—in fact, until its 2013 rebrand, the party was called the American Third Position Party.

Political Research Associates, a progressive group that tracks the extreme right, has described the Third Position movement as "a minor current of fascism" that borrows ideas liberally from both the extreme right and the extreme left. Its most important antecedent is Strasserism, a strain of Nazism that Adolf Hitler violently extinguished while consolidating his power in the thirties. Strasserists—named after the brothers Otto and Gregor Strasser— expounded a form of Nazi ideology that wedded scientific racism and conspiratorial anti-Semitism to radical anti-capitalism. Effectively, they put the "Socialism" in "National Socialism."

Hitler had Gregor and other prominent Strasserists murdered in the 1934 purge known as the Night of the Long Knives. Otto fled Germany, and lived in exile until 1974. But during the latter half of the twentieth century, other Third Position groups sprang up in Italy, France, and elsewhere. One of the most prominent Third Position offshoots was the Russian National Bolshevik Party, founded in 1994 and formally banned in 2007, which fused neo-fascism with nostalgia for Stalinist Communism. An early adopter of National Bolshevism, the right-wing political theorist Aleksandr Dugin, now enjoys friendly relations with both the Kremlin and America's white nationalist "alt-right."

Third Position ideologues tend to be impressed with their own originality, but fascists have always borrowed from the left when it suited them. Benito Mussolini—the fascist leader *par excellence*—began his career in politics as a scribbler for various socialist publications; he would go on to smuggle elements of socialist thought into a right-wing, nationalist framework. Nor was he alone, according to Barnard College political scientist Sheri Berman.

"During the interwar period, social democrats, fascists, and national socialists championed a 'third way' in economics that avoided the extremes of free-market liberalism and communism, insisting that the state could and should control capitalism without destroying it. ... The main difference was that under Fascists and Nazis, the price to pay for this program was the destruction of democracy and the jettisoning of civil liberties and human rights that accompanied it," wrote Berman in *The Primary of Politics,* her book on European social democracy.

THE MISSISSIPPI FREEDOM DEMOCRATIC PARTY

Formed in 1964 by civil rights activists to desegregate the Mississippi Democratic Party and the all-white delegation it sent to the Democratic National Convention that year.

The so-called Freedom Democrats elected their own delegates and sent them to the convention too. Group members, including activist Fannie Lou Hamer, testified before the DNC's credentials committee about the violence, threats and overall discrimination they faced. (Her remarks became legendary: "I am sick and tired of being sick and tired.")

The effort put pressure on President Lyndon B. Johnson, who needed the South—and the support of black leaders—for his re-election bid. Johnson offered the Freedom Democrats two seats in the delegation in exchange for the political support of the Rev. Martin Luther King Jr. and his organization, the Southern Christian Leadership Conference. But the Freedom Democrats rejected the deal because their two seats would have no voting power.

By some historical accounts, their refusal to take the seats amounted to a failure and later encouraged the rise of the more radical black power movement.

However, there's plenty of evidence that the Freedom Democrats succeeded. Their depiction of voter disenfranchisement and intimidation in Mississippi gained national sympathy that helped pave the way for the 1965 passage of the Voting Rights Act.

"Identity Politics: A Brief History," by Corey Dade, NPR, July 12, 2011.

Though the biggest difference between Third Positionism and other strands of fascism may be little more than a matter of emphasis, it is nonetheless an important distinction. Far more than many other white supremacist radicals, early Third Position devotees grasped the usefulness of fascism's political malleability. And by deliberately adopting left-wing vocabulary for some of their ideas, they presaged American white supremacism's return to the rhetoric of blue collar populism—something which Dixiecrats had embraced in the first half of the twentieth century, but gradually abandoned as they shifted into the Republican coalition.

Groups like the National Bolshevik Party and American Third Position can now plausibly claim to have been ahead of their time. They saw, better than nearly anyone else, how even a symbolic gesture toward left-wing economic thought could radically expand white nationalism's recruitment prospects.

But Third Positionism nonetheless spent decades on the fringes of the fringe. Until the liberal order's weakness gave them an opening.

The "Anti-anti-white left"

A movement becomes particularly vulnerable to subversion when it lacks both organizational discipline and strong intellectual leadership. That's the grim lesson being taught to us by Jeremy Corbyn.

When members of the UK's Labour Party first elected Corbyn as their leader in September 2015, progressive commentators on both sides of the Atlantic proclaimed a new dawn for the democratic socialism. A former union official and longtime backbencher, Corbyn seemed at first glance like an ideal champion for social democratic values. His election was also a stunning rebuke to former Labour PM Tony Blair, the person most responsible for turning what was once a leftist party of the working class into a vehicle for Third Way economics.

But if Labour was no longer the party of Blair, then what was it? There was certainly no going back to the days of blue collar social democracy that Corbyn seemed to represent. Decades after the right-wing Thatcher government and New Labour's neoliberal turn, the party's traditional union infrastructure had been entirely hollowed out. On top of that, the Scottish National Party had effectively routed Labour in its onetime electoral stronghold of Scotland. The party Corbyn remembered from his youth was dead.

What Labour did have—thanks to excitement over Corbyn and a rules change that made it easier to join—was hundreds of thousands of new members. But these freshman Labourites were skewing the party's demographics even further away from the working class that Corbyn claimed to represent. A January 2016 report on the incoming Labour membership found that "high-status city dwellers living in central locations and pursuing careers with high rewards are highly over-represented."

Without an industrial base, a disciplined trade union movement, or a coherent economic critique, the party has little to hold itself together besides Corbyn's appeal as a cult hero. In the words of British philosopher John Gray: "The defining feature of Corbynite Labour is not an anachronistic utopian socialism, but a very modern kind of liberal narcissism."

Recent British history has proven that such narcissism is powerless against a sustained right-wing assault. Although Labour was officially against Brexit, Corbyn's public efforts on behalf of Remain were perfunctory at best, and more than one-third of the party's supporters ultimately voted Leave. Now Labour is hemorrhaging votes to UKIP, prompting one prominent MP to observe that there are "no safe Labour seats" anymore.

The Democrats are not yet in such dire shape. The United States has a radically different party system and demographic makeup, making a total Labour-style collapse unlikely. But just as Blair's New Labour was a close cousin to Clinton's New Democrats, the pathologies of Corbynite Labour do have close American parallels.

Since the 1970s, both the United States and the United Kingdom have seen a precipitous decline in labor union strength and membership, facilitated in no small part by the negligence (and, sometimes, overt hostility) of center-left political leaders. The main result of this decline has been decades of wage stagnation for the Anglo-American working class. Its other consequences have been subtler, but no less dangerous.

Organized labor used to play a major role in structuring the politics of the working class and channeling its political energies. They were a crucial mediating institution between the Democratic Party and unionized workers, lobbying the party on behalf of its members while ensuring that those same members would support the party at the grassroots level. This system used to be particularly strong in the Rust Belt. That is where its decline been most dramatic.

The emaciation of Rust Belt organized labor left white workers in states like Michigan and Wisconsin politically adrift. The structure once provided by unions and similar communitarian institutions was superseded by another, more primal bond: white identity. It wasn't until the 2016 that the full consequences of this transformation became apparent, because no modern Republican candidate had fully exploited it before Trump. But on November 8, white Rust Belt workers surged to the polls and delivered the candidate of white populism an historic victory.

As the Rust Belt has entered a new political era, some "moderate" Democratic officeholders have followed. The most prominent example so far is Sen. Joe Manchin of West Virginia. After Trump won that state by more than forty points, Manchin immediately began signaling his willingness to collaborate with the president-elect, even going so far as to consider a cabinet position within the Trump administration. Though cable news will no doubt interpret Manchin's flirtation with the Republican White House as "centrism," the truth is American politics no longer has a center. Politicians either side with white populism or they don't. Manchin has made his choice; he won't be the last Democratic official to do so.

The erosion of liberal communitarianism didn't just abandon the former political center to the charms of white populism. It also created a new generation of white activists and thinkers who were bereft of ties to anything greater than their own expressive energies. Organized labor's decay meant fewer plausible career paths for aspiring activists; the simultaneous decline of professional stability in higher education has limited the possibilities for new ideas and rigorous scholarship from a left-wing perspective.

Alienated from any productive conduit for their political energies, and contemptuous of a Democratic Party they still associate with Third Way Clintonism, many white leftists have turned inward, toward an imagined past. Like Corbyn's base, they are in thrall to a politically sterile hodgepodge of cultural signifiers, coated in the thick musk of an idealized Old Left. Though some of those cultural signifiers might have seemed naïve or ridiculous in more innocent times, they are, in fact, eerily proximate to Third Position mythology. A small but significant chunk of the white left are closer than they know to right-wing nationalism.

For one thing, there's the shared nostalgia for past anti-democratic movements. Though not everyone on the anti-capitalist left romanticizes authoritarian regimes, an alarmingly large percentage of socialist thinkers and publications regularly indulge their proclivity for Soviet kitsch. These flights of fancy usually proceed from the base assumption that because American imperialism is bad, the forces that oppose it must therefore be good. Thus CounterPunch has published articles defending the Khmer Rouge; and, in a bizarre turn, the Green Party's 2016 presidential candidate wound up defending Russia's annexation of Crimea as a necessary response to an attempted Western "coup."

The usual defense of populist despots—of all persuasions—is that they're not anti-democratic because they represent the authentic will of the people. But it is exactly this claim that makes populism of both the left and the right inhospitable to democracy. As the political theorist Jann-Werner Müller has argued, when populists say they represent "the people," they are claiming "a moral monopoly of representation" that paints all disagreement as illegitimate. To populists of both the left and right, there is no good faith opposition; there are only enemies of the authentic people, however one chooses to define that term. White populists define it as a unified white nation.

In the American populist tradition, the "authentic people" are usually white workers. There exists a surprising left-right consensus that white workers have been "left behind" by the economy and the Democratic Party, even as people of color continue to make advances. The reality is somewhat different: As wealth inequality has grown steeper, households of color have suffered the most. And 2016 Democratic presidential candidate Hillary Clinton—identified as a candidate of the Third Way mainly because her husband is Bill Clinton—put forward a policy agenda that would have distributed significant amounts of wealth to the entire working class, white people included.

White workers have not been abandoned to their fate, but they constitute a smaller-than-ever portion of the working class as a whole. And thanks to a combination of changing demographics and civil rights legislation, they have lost some of the prerogatives of whiteness when it comes to things like hiring disparities and access to public goods. To stop "leaving behind" white workers would mean to reify America's caste system so they can regain those privileges. The white nationalists of the "alt-right" understand this and make it explicit. On the white left, it remains subtext.

But there's no need for subtext when it comes to describing the common enemies of the white left and populist right: black and brown "social justice warriors" and Clintonian centrism, which often get depicted as natural allies and enemies of the white working class. The left-wing version of this critique argues that "SJWs" insist on the primacy of "identity politics"—by which they mean any analysis that foregrounds issues of race, gender, and orientation, instead of calling them adjuncts to the labor question—and thereby strengthen neoliberalism by distracting everyone from the real issues. As an editor for the socialist journal Jacobin put it in May, "when racism can be blamed, capitalism can be exonerated." (Full disclosure: The author of this piece has written for Jacobin once in the past and knows socially several people affiliated with it.)

That Jacobin piece was cited approvingly in an essay called "The Anti-Anti-White Left" and published in December by the white supremacist website American Renaissance. The author of the American Renaissance post, Chris Roberts, defined the anti-anti-white left as "socialists who oppose racial identity politics generally and the shaming of poor whites in particular."

"Needless to say, they are not race realists or white advocates, and they openly abhor what they call 'racism,'" wrote Roberts. "However, they are so preoccupied with economics and class that they have little respect for theories about 'white privilege,' or 'authoritarian personalities.'"

Roberts ended his essay by wondering aloud whether "one in four of these anti-anti-white socialists could become white advocates." It is perhaps worth noting that the editor of American Renaissance is Jared Taylor, an ally of the American Third Position movement.

No Pasarán

White nationalist ideology is powerful enough to bridge the left-right divide, but it is not yet powerful enough to command an electoral majority. Donald Trump lost the popular vote, and he is currently the most unpopular president-elect in the history of modern polling. Whatever their individual prejudices, most Americans want to live in a multiracial democracy.

But that democracy is under threat. White nationalists understand they can't win a fair election, so they will spent the next four years trying to render more elections either unfair or irrelevant. They're already well along in North Carolina, where the Republican legislature has moved to strip power from the incoming Democratic governor. In any state they can, white populists will soon take further steps to hobble the offices they don't control and suppress non-white votes.

They have power, but not numbers. In order to stop them, supporters of pluralist democracy will need to assemble a mass movement that reaches into every community, every state capital, and every congressional office it can. The existing liberal infrastructure in most states is not what it once was, but activists will need it as a starting point to rebuild newer, stronger networks. Most of the important work will be done on the state and local level. Labor unions, houses of worship, and community groups all have key roles to play.

Under no circumstances should this movement back away from its commitment to pluralism. The aim of white nationalism is to destroy the multiracial democratic state, and any attempt at compromise will only bring it closer to that goal. People of color, women, LGBT people, and members of other marginalized groups are not a liability to the resistance against Trump; they are its leaders.

If the North Carolina GOP has charted the way forward for white populism, the state's Moral Mondays movement has done the same for multiracial democracy. That movement, led by state NAACP president Rev. William Barber II, is one of the most vital and important protest campaigns in modern American history. Recent polling suggests it was the key ingredient that toppled Republican Gov. Pat McCrory in the 2016 election, prompting the state legislature's attempt to kneecap his successor. The Moral Mondays movement succeeded by capitalizing on its own diversity, not apologizing for it.

As *The Atlantic*'s Vann R. Newkirk II wrote after the election, the movement "expanded its ranks not by appealing to a class-based ethos, but by casting economic, social, and political issues as moral dilemmas and emphasizing empathy." Rev. Barber knitted together a motley group of Black Lives Matter activists, union members, pro-choice protesters, LGBT advocates, DREAMers, and more. But his coalition didn't just transcend divisions within the progressive advocacy world; it also spoke to people across the left-right political spectrum, using the language of morality, democracy, and community. And in an exceedingly dark year, it won a critical victory.

Keeping the promise of multiracial democracy does not mean ignoring white workers. But instead of abandoning core values in a misbegotten attempt to win them over, liberals can peel them off by exploiting weaknesses in Trump's coalition. The president-elect won thanks to an uneasy alliance of white populists, robber barons, and laissez faire ideologues; in the time before his inauguration, internal disagreements over matters like health care and retirement security have already strained that alliance.

Early reports suggest that the incoming Senate Democratic leader, New York's Chuck Schumer, will attempt to drive a wedge between congressional Republicans and the White House by facilitating Trump's less conservative economic plans. That would be a grievous mistake. Instead of dividing Trump from his party, Schumer would be better served doing everything in his power to yoke them together. The Tea Party's economic agenda is still wildly unpopular, and Trump should not have the luxury of distance from it.

Trump is beatable. So is the white nationalist tide he rode to office. But however the next few years shake out, there will be no going back to liberal democratic order of Bill Clinton, or even of Barack Obama. If liberalism emerges from this trial, it will be fundamentally changed.

How it will change is impossible to predict. But remember that a previous crisis of democracy birthed the present global order, the one that is now splintering apart. The dangers of the 1930s were even greater than the threats of the present era: they included totalitarianism, genocide, and an unprecedented global depression. Those pressures transformed liberal democracy. But they did not break it.

Today, democracy faces another storm. If it weathers this one, it might well emerge stronger than ever, much as it did in the post-war era. But for that to happen, it will need all the reinforcements it can get.

> *"Both the president-elect and his chief strategist have publicly disavowed white nationalism, but the campaign they rode to the White House has undeniably emboldened the nationalist movement."*

White Nationalism Is Becoming More Accepted in the United States

Alexis Terrazas and Atticus Morris

In the following viewpoint, Alexis Terrazas and Atticus Morris profile a young Marine named Nathan Damigo as he has become increasingly influenced by the white nationalist movement. While serving time in prison for armed robbery, after returning home from Iraq with post-traumatic stress disorder, Damigo became initiated into the so-called "identitarian movement." According to Damigo, "identitarians" are not looking to kill or hurt anyone, as racist groups such as the Ku Klux Klan have done in the past, but are focused on political organizing according to race and identity—and particularly white, European identity. Through their interview with Damigo, the authors excavate the worrisome popularity of such white nationalist groups, especially among young men. Terrazas is editor in chief of El Tecolote. Morris is web and social media manager at Accion Latina.

"Alternate Reality: Growing Acceptance of White Nationalism In Trump's America," by Alexis Terrazas and Atticus Morris, Eltecolote, December 15, 2016. Reprinted by permission.

As you read, consider the following questions:

1. Nathan Damigo labels himself an "identitarian." What does this mean?
2. How do figures like David Duke appeal to certain groups of people, including Nathan Damigo?
3. What is "anti-white hate speech" according to Damigo?

Sitting in his study surrounded by dozens of books, Nathan Damigo is roughly 100 pages into his latest literary venture, "Why We Fight: Manifesto of the European Resistance," by Guillaume Faye.

"It's great," he said in an interview with El Tecolote, via facetime. "Give it a read. I think you'll find it insightful." Damigo, a self-described "Identitarian" and founder of the Oakdale, California-based white nationalist group "Identity Evropa," wasn't always a reader. He developed the habit, which he now considers a "healthy obsession," while serving four years in prison for armed robbery.

"I don't remember it horribly well, but I remember it well enough," Damigo said of the night that changed his life.

He was 21 and had recently returned home from his second tour of duty as a Marine in Iraq.

On Nov. 11, 2007, Corporal Nathan Benjamin Damigo robbed Changiz Ezzatyar, a San Diego cab driver, at gunpoint.

"It's something that I'm certainly not proud of," said Damigo, who is now 30. "When I got back from Iraq, I was having some major issues."

Court documents obtained by El Tecolote show Damigo was diagnosed with having PTSD by three different doctors, and was charged with a felony count of robbery, and a misdemeanor count of carrying a concealed weapon. On Jan. 26, 2010, Damigo pleaded guilty to felony robbery; he was sentenced to six years in prison on Feb. 26, 2010.

Damigo likened his time in prison to a "four-year sabbatical," and said that his "red pill" awakening moment (a reference from the film "The Matrix") came sometime in 2011 when he read a book by prominent white supremacist David Duke, the former Imperial Wizard of the Ku Klux Klan.

"I actually kind of read it as a joke. And was like, 'Oh wow, there's a lot of interesting stuff here,'" he said. "I think [Duke] is a man who was willing to say things that weren't politically correct. It was very easy to demonize him to the general public."

Though Damigo acknowledges that he identified with other whites in prison, he claims that's not what influenced his current views.

"It was my time in prison, but it wasn't. It was the fact that I had time to sit and reflect and think and study and read. That's what it was that led me to my beliefs," Damigo said. "In California prison, every race goes with their own race. That's simply how it is. So yeah, I was with the other whites."

Damigo's older brother, Josh, however, believes his alliance with whites in prison did influence his views.

He became a member of the "white gangs while in jail, as a survival tactic," Josh Damigo wrote in an email to El Tecolote. "I believe this was a huge disservice to him, since he needed help for PTSD, not jail time. [District Attorney] Bonnie Dumanis and the City of San Diego did him and all Marines a terrible disservice by convicting him."

From 'Skater Boy' to White Nationalist

Damigo's journey from "skater boy" to combat Marine veteran, and from an ex-con to a prominent white nationalist, begins in San Jose, CA where he was raised.

According to a psychological evaluation, Damigo was diagnosed with ADHD at age 8 and began taking Ritalin. He stopped when he reached high school at Liberty Baptist, a small private Christian school on San Jose's south side.

"It was really f***ing diverse," Damigo said of Liberty Baptist. "Everyone was a minority."

According to the evaluation, he had learning disabilities in high school, required a special tutor and took special education classes for two years at Liberty Baptist, where his mother was a teacher and principal.

He joined the Marines in November, 2004, during his senior year. A corporal in the First Light Armored Reconnaissance Battalion, Damigo was deployed to western Iraq for seven months from August 2005 to March 2006.

During his deployment, two of his close friends were killed, one by an improvised explosive device attack and the other in a firefight. Wrought with grief and survivor guilt, when he returned he began drinking heavily and eventually attempted suicide. He did not seek help after the attempt.

Damigo was deployed for a second tour in early 2007 and, despite exhibiting symptoms of PTSD, he excelled. When he returned home in October 2007 his symptoms continued to worsen.

"He was always the more likable kid in my family, but when he came home, he was just different—more calculated, less loving," wrote his brother Josh. "We were roommates when he got back from Iraq ... He suddenly wanted a baseball bat at the door of the house for 'safety,' and was much more nervous and 'cautious' when he came back. It didn't make much sense to me."

In November 2007, near the anniversary of his deceased friend, Lance Cpl. Jeremy Tamburello, Damigo began drinking heavily while alone in his brother Josh's San Diego apartment. He had planned to end his life using a pistol, but instead decided to take a walk to clear his head. His walk led him to a park in La Mesa, where he encountered the taxi driver, Changiz Ezzatyar.

According to Damigo's first psychological evaluation by clinical psychologist Heidi S. Kraft on Dec. 5, 2007, Damigo admitted that the decision was a poor one, but he believed it might make him "feel alive."

In a neuropsychological evaluation by Barbara J. Schrock dated June 23–24, 2008, Damigo said he was sure Ezzatyar was Iraqi.

"He reported that because he thought he [Ezzatyar] was Iraqi, 'I wanted to kill the dude,'" read Schrock's evaluation. Damigo forced Ezzatyar to the ground at gunpoint and told him to give him his money. He then walked to the end of the block, realized what he had done, and started running.

Damigo's mental health continued to deteriorate over the course of 2008–09, as he abused drugs and alcohol and again attempted suicide. During this period, he underwent multiple psychological evaluations, but gave conflicting accounts of the robbery. In one account he claimed he had experienced a flashback, believing he was back in Iraq when he robbed Ezzatyar.

One conclusion that remained consistent throughout his evaluations was that Damigo's intelligence was above average and that he exhibited leadership in the military.

Forming a New Identity

After being released from prison in 2014, and armed with his new radical ideology, Damigo co-founded a white nationalist group called National Youth Front with the help of someone he found online. But the venture fizzled due in part to a copyright infringement with a Christian youth organization called "Youth Front."

He continued to publicize his nationalist views on a blog called "Dispossessedtemp," until launching Identity Evropa in March 2016.

On Oct. 17, Damigo and about a dozen of Identity Evropa members held an anti-immigration rally at Pier 14, calling for an end to San Francisco's sanctuary city policy.

Identity Evropa, which now has more than 100 members according to Damigo, bears little resemblance to the classic image of white supremacists—no white hoods, no shaved heads, no swastika tattoos or racial slurs. They are well-groomed, well-dressed and well-spoken.

"We're not looking to intimidate people," Damigo said. "That's not what our purpose is. We're focused on one thing, which is race and identity."

To Damigo and his group this means advocating for a moratorium on immigration—both legal and "illegal"— for anyone who isn't of European ancestry, and dividing the United States into racially segregated "ethnostates."

"We reject [the idea of] multiracialism as being something that is good for European people," Damigo said. "Do we want to have this person breeding in our gene pool?"

Damigo claims that these sorts of ideas are not in fact racist and that labeling them so constitutes "anti-white hate speech" that is used to undermine "European interests."

Membership to Identity Evropa is strictly limited to people who can trace their ancestry to Europe, except for Jews, who are prohibited even if they have European ancestry. Damigo also doesn't allow members to date interracially, calling it "selfish," although he once almost married an ex-girlfriend, who is Latina.

He doesn't however see a problem in indulging in non-European cuisine or enjoying other cultures.

"European people have been doing that for a long time … there's nothing wrong with that. If it's a unit of culture that is good … Why can't we adopt that into our culture?" he said. "What I'm rejecting is a system that is problematic. Multiracialism creates conflict within a society."

These kinds of ideas and the people and organizations that promote them such as Identity Evropa, are part of what has become known as the "alt-right."

The So-called "Alt-right"

Coined by a white nationalist named Richard Spencer, the alternative right or "alt-right" isn't so much an actual group as it is a catch-all term applied to a diffuse collection of people who share a common set of ideas. The "alternative" refers to a rejection of classic conservatism's focus on economics and foreign policy, in favor of an ideology based around identity—specifically white, straight, male identity. The movement can be best understood as a backlash to multiculturalism. It includes traditional far-right conservatives, anti-Semites, anti-immigration activists, Internet provocateurs, men's rights activists and old-school racists as well as white nationalists like Damigo and Spencer.

The people who've adopted this label believe among other things that traditional conservatism has been hijacked by global elites, that reverse-racism is real, that it is Christians who are being persecuted for their religious beliefs and that a "culture of political correctness" is the greatest threat to personal liberty. They also happen to believe that Western Civilization is superior to all others and that it is inseparable from European identity.

The Associated Press, which governs journalism writing conventions, has labeled the term "alt-right" a "public relations device," suggesting that it deliberately obscures the controversial views of people like Spencer and Damigo. "In the past we have called such beliefs racist, neo-Nazi or white supremacist," wrote John Daniszewski, AP's vice president for standards.

Spencer, a sharply dressed, soft-spoken intellectual, has also adopted the "identitarian" label. He currently heads the National Policy Institute (NPI), a Washington, DC-based white nationalist think tank.

"America, at the end of the day belongs to white men," he proclaimed recently in a lecture he gave at Texas A & M.

A New Era for White Nationalism

The ideas that individuals like Damigo and Spencer advocate have, of course, been part of America's political landscape since the early days of the Ku Klux Klan. They are typically relegated to the margins of political discourse, but can gain traction from time to time, usually in periods of social upheaval. And the rise of Donald Trump has provided such an upheaval.

Trump's foray into politics began in 2012 when he led the "birthers," a movement built around a baseless conspiracy theory designed to delegitimize the nation's first black president. In June of 2015, when he officially threw his hat in the ring for president, he marked the occasion by giving a racist speech degrading Mexican immigrants, which played directly to the identity politics of white nationalism. Over the course of his path to the presidency, Trump styled himself as the candidate of "law and order," threatening to crackdown on racial justice groups like Black Lives Matter; he promised to deport millions of undocumented immigrants and build a wall along the U.S.-Mexico border; and he threatened to ban Muslims from entering the country.

He also helped push white nationalist propaganda through his Twitter account, by sharing content such as a false report about "black on white" crime that originated from Neo-Nazi sources, and an altered image of Hillary Clinton behind a six-pointed star of David and a pile of cash reading "Most corrupt candidate ever" (which was roundly condemned as anti-semitic).

"Donald Trump's campaign was the first step toward identity politics in the United States," Spencer told reporters during a recent NPI conference in Washington, DC. Spencer added that while he didn't consider Trump to be "alt-right," per se, the president-elect more than any other republican shared a "psychic" connection with the movement.

Trump's choice of Stephen Bannon as his chief strategist and senior counselor is considered by many to be a blatant nod to the "alt-right." Bannon was a founding board member and former executive chair of controversial Breitbart.com, the conservative website known for its toxic ideologically-driven style of partisan journalism. Bannon famously called Breitbart "the platform for the 'alt-right.'"

Since assuming his new role, Bannon has sought to distance himself from white nationalism, but not specifically the "alt-right."

Ben Shapiro, a former Breitbart reporter, who left earlier this year because of Bannon's close ties with the Trump campaign, described Bannon in an interview with Slate.com as "very power-hungry," and said he is "willing to use anybody and anything in order to get ahead, and that includes making common cause with the racist, anti-Semitic alt-right."

Both the president-elect and his chief strategist have publicly disavowed white nationalism, but the campaign they rode to the White House has undeniably emboldened the nationalist movement, has thrust the issue of white identity to the forefront of the political discussion, and in the process has given men like Damigo and Spencer a platform they could have only dreamed of a few years ago.

Damigo said he doesn't consider Trump to be a part of the movement, but he said the president-elect's upset victory over Hillary Clinton "was a big deal for us."

"The thing that I liked about him [Trump] was he created space to have a conversation, he put things like immigration back on the table," he said. "Whether or not he's going to fulfill his promises, I'm skeptical. If he goes back on his word, we're going to be going after him harder than anyone else."

Periodical and Internet Sources Bibliography

The following articles have been selected to supplement the diverse views presented in this chapter.

Corey Dade, "Identity Politics: A Brief History," *NPR*, July 12, 2011, http://www.npr.org/2011/07/12/137789802/identity-politics-a-brief-history.

David French, "On MLK Day, Stand Against Identity Politics," *National Review*, January 16, 2017, http://www.nationalreview.com/article/443891/martin-luther-king-day-identity-politics-does-not-honor-his-legacy.

Josh Harkinson, "Trump Selects a White Nationalist Leader as a Delegate in California, *Mother Jones*, August 2016, http://www.motherjones.com/politics/2016/05/donald-trump-white-nationalist-afp-delegate-california.

Kim Holmes, "Why Identity Politics Is Causing a War Among Feminists," *Daily Signal*, February 9, 2016, http://dailysignal.com/2016/02/09/why-identity-politics-is-causing-a-war-among-feminists.

James M. Jasper and Aidan McGarry, "Introduction: *The Identity Dilemma, Social Movements, and Contested Identity,*" Temple University Press, http://www.temple.edu/tempress/chapters_1800/2364_ch1.pdf.

Laila Lalami, "The Identity Politics of Whiteness," *New York Times*, November 21, 2016, https://www.nytimes.com/2016/11/27/magazine/the-identity-politics-of-whiteness.html.

Walter Benn Michaels et al., "What Is the Left Without Identity Politics?" *Nation*, December 16, 2016, https://www.thenation.com/article/what-is-the-left-without-identity-politics.

Stanford Encyclopedia of Philosophy, "Identity Politics," July 16, 2002, https://plato.stanford.edu/entries/identity-politics.

Tabitha Southey, "Flipping the Script on History: Identity Politics 101," *Globe and Mail*, January 27, 2017, https://www.theglobeandmail.com/opinion/flipping-the-script-on-history-identity-politics-101/article33803778.

Vanessa Williams, "An Identity Crisis for Identity Politics," *Washington Post*, July 27, 2017, https://www.washingtonpost.com/news/post-nation/wp/2017/07/27/an-identity-crisis-for-identity-politics.

OPPOSING
VIEWPOINTS®
SERIES

CHAPTER 2

How Has Identity Politics Incorporated or Ignored Intersectionality?

Chapter Preface

Identity politics has been lauded for allowing marginalized groups of people to have a voice and a role in government. It also has been criticized for focusing on fixed and exclusive, rather than inclusive, identities. One of the loudest criticisms against identity politics revolves around the issue of intersectionality. "Intersectionality" is a term that explains how every piece of our identity affects who we are. Thus, a white woman from a wealthy family in the northeastern United States has a very different lived experience than a white woman from a poor family in the rural South. Thus, race, ethnicity, class, gender, and sexual orientation all *intersect* to inform who we are and how we self-identify.

In this chapter, we will explore viewpoints that have to do with how intersectionality is used or misused within identity politics. Beverly Amsel, a psychologist, starts off the chapter with a discussion of how fixed and immutable identities create rifts in families. According to Amsel, identity politics forms divisions around people rather than focusing on their commonalities.

Next, Julia Serano and Hugh Ryan write about how exclusive identity politics has become in the feminist and queer movements, respectively. For these authors, a simplistic way of interpreting identity politics can lead to rifts within groups if people do not fit in with a particular, stringent identity.

Maria Murriel examines the white ethno-nationalist movement in the United States to explore how intersectionality can be used to great—or detrimental—effect within political organizing.

Many of the authors featured in this chapter disagree, although they tend to agree on one main point: inclusion rather than exclusion is integral to a fully functional identity politics.

> *"With this binary thrust upon us by political events and social conditions, our human, emotional identities are being erased in our relationships."*

There Are Psychological Consequences to Identity Politics

Beverly Amsel

In the following viewpoint, Beverly Amsel speaks about the psychological consequences of "identity politics," particularly when it creates divisions among family members. She suggests how identity politics can harm family life and how families who share different political identities might come together and heal their relationships. For Amsel, empathy—and not strict political divisions— "opens up the possibility of seeing and relating to the other as a unique, human person, not just a member of a social or political category." Amsel is a licensed psychotherapist who writes for GoodTherapy.org.

"'Who Am I?': Identity Politics and Family Conflict," by Beverly Amsel, GoodTherapy.org, January 10, 2017. Reprinted by permission.

As you read, consider the following questions:

1. How does the author define identity politics?
2. How does the author answer this question: "How can I help people…shape positive identities and better tolerate their families' aggression so they don't have to choose between (1) accepting the shame and rejection from their family for political choices, or (2) possibly severing ties with them?"
3. How can empathy and understanding help solve conflicts brought about by identity politics, according to the viewpoint?

For the first time in over 20 years, the events in the political and social world have entered my consulting room in a way that is not only troubling, but also problematic to address. Anxiety is on the rise. It has been my experience that "identity politics," the divisions and conflicts that have intensified in our society during and since the election, are creating severe disruptions not simply between anonymous people with differing political affiliations, but more importantly for the work I do, in relationships between family members, friends, and coworkers.

Political pundits and social media describe our social divisions in terms of identity politics: conflicts are occurring between people with different racial, social class, gender, and other social identities. We pigeonhole people, then assign them to polarized identity groups with the choice of identity narrowed to the binary of "us" and "them." With this binary thrust upon us by political events and social conditions, our human, emotional identities are being erased in our relationships.

In my psychotherapy office, conflicts around identity have emerged as a major focus in therapy sessions. Since the election, I hear a lot of talk about "us" and "them" as I listen to some people talk about themselves and their relationships in the world. One person, Christopher, spoke of a painful Thanksgiving dinner where his father told him, "I'm ashamed of you! How could you vote for that criminal Hillary? You're not one of us."

Separately, Liz, someone who assumed I supported the Democratic nominee, was reluctant to acknowledge she supported Donald Trump. Nevertheless, after a haranguing phone call from her mother, who supported Hillary Clinton, she came to her session so full of feelings that she risked talking to me about the encounter. She sobbed as she told me:

"I really didn't want to bring up the election because I think you're for Hillary. But I don't think you're a fanatic like my mother, and I can't stand these horrible feelings. I think she hates me. She called me and screamed that I better not vote for Trump. She said, 'No daughter of mine could be so stupid and ignorant. You're an embarrassment.'"

Identity and Its Development

What, exactly, is identity? It is not a simplistic notion built on who we vote for and social categories such as class, race, and gender. Nor is it just other socially identifying categories: father, churchgoer, ping-pong player, Boy Scout. While it can include all of the above, it is a much more complex notion based on the answer to the question: "Who am I?"

The answer to this question begins to develop in early childhood. The family provides the foundation for the development of a sense of self. When parents mirror their children by reflecting back the child's thoughts and feelings, the child feels heard and known. This is an important building block in the development of self-esteem, self-worth, and identity. Eventually, as the child separates and individuates from their parents, they begin to define themselves as they construct their answers to the "who am I?" question.

Central to identity and sense of self is an emotional orientation to "who am I?" Thus, I can be proud of what I work at, scared of being a parent, hopeless about success, disappointed about my life, grateful for my opportunities, ashamed, resentful, jealous, loving, hateful, etc. All of these self-states, and many more, comprise my identity.

Ideally, throughout life, we become free to independently reflect on and develop our sense of self as it is constructed in the conscious and unconscious interactions that occur in all our relationships. But not everyone is fortunate enough to grow up with the tools to be able to develop a unique sense of self. Separation and individuation can be compromised by demands to adhere to the family's definitions of what is acceptable and unacceptable. As a consequence, attempts at self-definition that depart from family norms can lead to uncomfortable and intolerable feelings that interfere with the ability to know who one is and what one wants. Identities that are stuck in family definitions are not fluid, and typically require self-validation from an outside audience.

When the development of identity has historically adhered rigidly to family requirements, one is more vulnerable to seeing identities as inflexible and unalterable. This orientation can lead to viewing the world as the binary "us" and "them."

With identity politics having a strong impact on many of the people I work with in therapy, I ask myself: "How can I help people like Christopher and Liz shape positive identities and better tolerate their families' aggression so they don't have to choose between (1) accepting the shame and rejection from their family for political choices, or (2) possibly severing ties with them?"

Both Christopher and Liz felt under assault by their parents. They were in disbelief that their parents could lash out so forcefully. Christopher was very angry at his father: "He's so rigid and closed-minded. I can't have an intelligent conversation with him. I never thought I'd think of my father as a bigot or stupid, but that's what I'm thinking now. I don't like these feelings. I keep thinking, 'Does my mother agree? Am I a bad son?' "

I asked Christopher, "What would you like your father to understand about you? He told you that 'you're not one of us.' Is that how it feels to you?"

Christopher thought silently for a few minutes and responded: "I want my father to see I'm still his son. I may have different views about how government should be responsive to people and about women and gay people, but I'm a good human being and I've always been a good son. He gets to me. I feel so rejected and ashamed. But I'm angry, too. It's so confusing."

I then asked Christopher what he thought his father would say if I asked him what he'd like Christopher to understand about him. At first, Christopher replied he didn't know. But he thought for a bit and said:

"I guess he'd want me to see he's not a bigot or a racist. He wouldn't admit it, but he's probably scared. My mom's unemployed, and he hates his job and doesn't make enough money. He's getting old, and I suppose he feels pretty powerless. Maybe he wants me to know he's angry and disappointed about his life. I know I never think about him this way, but I suppose it's true. Maybe voting for Trump gives him hope. I think it's crazy, but I suppose he doesn't."

Talking with Christopher about his father's vote for Trump led us to hypothesize about and explore his father's fuller identity, rather than ascribe the binary identity of Trump supporter. It allowed Christopher to develop some empathy for his father's hurtful outburst to him on Thanksgiving. It also helped him to think about their different identities beyond "us" and "them."

While their political identities differed, Christopher talked about the ways in which he was similar and different in values to his father: "It's funny. We're both generous people. He's more socially conservative than I am, but we're both churchgoers; we volunteer. He's a wonderful grandfather to my son. He can be critical with people and was always somewhat harsh and critical with me. I've gotten better in not taking on his judgments. I'm still a little prone to being sensitive to criticism. He can lose his temper, which I never do. Still, he's been a pretty good role model for me in raising my son."

Knowing this, of course, is not enough to make peace between Christopher and his father. Fortunately, Christopher has individuated enough from his family to have internalized a sense of himself that feels valuable and confident. While he still occasionally is vulnerable to taking on and accepting criticism without carefully considering if it is applicable, for the most part he can maintain his positive sense of self in the face of threats like his father's Thanksgiving assault.

When Liz and I talked about her mother, a picture of a woman similar to Liz emerged: "We're both very passionate about things. As a kid, we heard about this woman that was mistreating her animals. Mom and I got very active in getting the animals taken away from her. We both still work for animal rights. When we don't agree, she can get nasty. I suppose I was pretty scared of her rages growing up. That awful phone call about my not voting for Hillary was a pretty typical communication. I guess I had a pretty typical response. I get angry and scared. I have an urge to comply, which would and wouldn't make me feel better. But I won't change my vote. I thought of lying to her about it."

Liz and I talked more about who her mother was as a person, not just a Hillary voter. Both she and Christopher got the point: their relationships with parents are complex and multilayered, with so much history. Voting for Trump or Clinton is not what defines who anyone is, nor does it have to divide a parent-child relationship into "us" and "them."

Having empathy, attempting to make sense of another person's political choices in light of who they are as people, can lead to an understanding and acceptance of the other's full identity, not the binary identity choice of Trump voter vs. Clinton voter, "us" and "them." In no way does having empathy mean one is condoning or agreeing with the other's choices. Rather, it opens up the possibility of seeing and relating to the other as a unique, human person, not just a member of a social or political category.

In my psychotherapy practice, people who have had more success individuating tend to be better able to overcome the anxieties created by the differences between themselves and their family members. They are more able to withstand the bad feelings that can result from being seen as an unacceptable other. When they can develop the capacity for empathy and understanding about their family members' political choices, the tensions and intolerable feelings between family members may diminish, become more tolerable, and binary thinking can be expanded.

It is my hope that, as a society, we can find a way to be more empathic toward people with opposing political views without constructing binary identities that create what feels like irresolvable conflict and aggression.

Note: *To protect privacy, names in the preceding article have been changed and the dialogues described are a composite.*

> *"I have found feminism to be an indispensable foundation for me to make sense of my experiences and to articulate the obstacles and issues that I face."*

Identity Politics Is a Good Thing That Can Be Destructive When Used to Exclude

Julia Serano

In the following viewpoint, Julia Serano argues that there are three "sides" of feminism, the emergence of which has led to tension within the movement because of differing identities. She uses the example of the Michigan Womyn's Music Festival (MWMF) to show how certain identities have been traditionally left out of feminism. In this case, organizers of this women-only event excluded trans women from participation, leading to rifts within the feminist movement at large and bringing up questions of identity, sexism, and privilege. Serano suggests that identity politics can be dangerous when it is used to exclude others who share similar political and social concerns. Serano is a writer, trans activist, and author of Excluded: Making Feminist and Queer Movements *(Seal Press, 2013) and* Whipping Girl: A Transsexual Woman on Sexism and the Scapegoating of Femininity *(Seal Press, 2007).*

"Rethinking Sexism: How Trans Women Challenge Feminism," by Julia Serano, Alternet, August 4, 2008. Reprinted by permission.

As you read, consider the following questions:

1. What are the three "sides" to the debate that Serano sets out?

2. Why have some lesbian-feminists suggested that trans women should not be included in their movement?

3. How might our understanding of identity politics shift based on Serano's definition of an inclusive feminism?

In 1991, Nancy Jean Burkholder was expelled from the Michigan Womyn's Music Festival (MWMF), the world's largest annual women-only event, because festival workers suspected that she was a trans woman—that is, someone who was assigned a male sex at birth but who identifies and lives as female. That incident sparked protests from a burgeoning transgender movement to challenge what eventually came to be known as the festival's "womyn-born-womyn"-only policy, which effectively bars trans women from attending. The protests evolved into Camp Trans, which continues to take place just down the road from MWMF each year, and which has become a focal point for a much broader push for trans-inclusion within feminist and queer communities. Despite more than 15 years of petitioning, and a growing acceptance of trans identities in both mainstream society and within queer, feminist and other progressive circles, the festival still officially maintains its "womyn-born-womyn"-only policy, and countless other lesbian- and queer-woman-focused groups and events continue to harbor dismissive, if not outright disdainful, attitudes toward trans women. The history of the MWMF trans woman-exclusion debate has been retold countless times—often in an overly simplistic, cut-and-dry manner. The controversy is usually depicted in one of two ways: either pitting the supposedly out-of-touch, transphobic lesbian-separatists who run the festival against a more politically progressive transgender minority, or portraying transgender activists as bullies who selfishly seek to undermine one of the few remaining vestiges of women-only space with their supposedly masculine bodies and energies. In addition to being obvious caricatures, these sorts of us-versus-them portrayals obscure one of the most important aspects of the story: the fact that there are actually three "sides" to this debate, each driven by a different take on feminism.

Rather than rehash the history or delve into all of the details about the festival and the controversy, I will attempt to describe these three differing feminist perspectives and discuss how they have played out with regard to the issue of trans woman-exclusion at MWMF, as well as in lesbian/queer women's communities more generally.

For those unfamiliar with the subject, I will start by defining some of the trans-specific language that I will be using. Transsexuals are individuals who identify and live as members of the sex other than the one they were assigned at birth. A trans woman is someone who has socially, physically and/or legally transitioned from male to female, and a trans man is someone who has similarly transitioned from female to male. While the medical establishment (and the mainstream media) typically define "transsexual" in terms of the medical procedures that an individual might undergo (for example, hormones and surgeries), many trans people find such definitions to be objectifying (as they place undue focus on body parts rather than the person as a whole) and classist (as not all trans people can afford to physically transition). For these reasons, trans activists favor definitions based on self-identity, that is, whether one identifies and lives as a woman or man. "Transgender" is an umbrella term for all people who defy other people's expectations and assumptions regarding gender, and can be used to refer to transsexuals as well as people who are gender nonconforming in other ways—for example, cross-dressers, drag performers, feminine men, masculine women, and genderqueers (who do not identify exclusively as either women or men), to name a few. Transgender people who defy gender norms in the male-to-female/feminine direction are said to be on the trans feminine spectrum; those who transgress gender norms in the female-to-male/masculine direction make up the trans masculine spectrum.

Unilateral Sexism and Lesbian-Feminism

MWMF is one of many women-only institutions that grew out of the lesbian-feminist movement during the 1970s and 1980s. A dominant ideology within that movement was the belief that sexism constitutes a unilateral form of oppression—that is, men are the oppressors, and women the oppressed, end of story. While more liberal or reform-minded feminists of that time period focused primarily on the most obvious examples of sexism (e.g., wage and workplace discrimination, sexual harassment, reproductive rights, etc.), lesbian- (and other radical) feminists extended their critiques of sexism to include many taken-for-granted aspects of gender and sexuality. They argued, for example, that masculinity is inherently dominating and oppressive and that femininity is necessarily associated with objectification and subjugation, and that both forms of gender expression are merely products of socialization rather than natural aspects of people. According to this perspective, a first step toward overturning sexism is for individuals to distance themselves from ways of being that are associated with male domination and female subjugation and instead revert to more natural (and presumably androgynous) forms of gender and sexual expression.

Lesbian-feminist critiques did not solely take aim at the heterosexual mainstream; they also targeted other sexual minorities whose gender and sexual practices were deemed (in their view) to emulate unilateral sexism. This includes those who engage in BDSM (who were seen as reinforcing dominant/submissive sexual roles), and butch and femme lesbians, drag performers, cross-dressers, and transsexuals (who were all seen as reinforcing masculine/feminine gender roles). While lesbian-feminists derided many forms of what we would now call transgender expression, the bulk of their contempt was directed squarely at trans women and others on the trans feminine spectrum. This attitude stemmed both from the assumption that trans women are "really men" (i.e., oppressors) and that femininity is tantamount to a "slave status." Thus, according to this logic, trans female and trans feminine individuals were viewed as oppressors who appropriate the dress and identities of the very people they oppress. For example, feminist Robin Morgan claimed that trans women "parody female oppression and suffering," and Mary Daly equated trans feminine expression with "whites playing "blackface."" Many (including Morgan and, most famously, Janice Raymond) even described trans womanhood as a form of rape.

While many lesbian-feminists today will concede that such accusations are beyond the pale, their unilateral perspective on sexism still leads them to insist that trans women should not be allowed to enter women-only spaces such as MWMF based on the assumption that trans women have experienced male socialization and privilege in the past, and/or because their bodies, personalities and energies still supposedly remain "male" or "masculine" on some level.

The Gender Binary, Queer Theory and Transgender Activism

Prior to the mid-1990s, trans women and allies typically responded to trans woman-exclusion by stressing the similarities between trans women (who live as women and thus experience misogyny in their day-to-day lives) and non-trans women. But this strategy of emphasizing similarities became less relevant by the mid-to-late 1990s due to the rise of "third wave" feminisms, which challenged universalizing views of womanhood and examined the many differences that exist between women. For example, "third wave" feminists embraced the critiques made by women of color over the years that the belief that sexism was the "primary" oppression, or even a unilateral form of oppression, ignores the ways in which sexism intersects with racism and classism in many women's lives. Additionally, many feminists (especially younger ones) around this time began reclaiming expressions of femininity and sexuality that had previously been considered taboo or repressive among lesbian-feminists. But perhaps no shift in feminism had such a profound affect on transgender-inclusion within lesbian and queer women's communities as the rise of queer theory.

Queer theory shares the lesbian-feminist belief that many aspects of gender and sexuality are culturally derived (rather than natural), but takes this notion one step further by bringing into question the very categories upon which sexisms are based. This is often accomplished by critiquing, subverting and deconstructing the "gender binary"—that is, the assumption that there are only two legitimate genders: feminine women and masculine men. For this reason, many queer theorists became particularly interested in transgender people, whom they sometimes hailed for challenging traditional notions about femaleness and maleness. This view is in sharp contrast to lesbian-feminist perspectives, which claimed that these same individuals reinforced oppressive sex roles.

Queer theory both influenced, and was influenced by, the rise of transgender activism—a movement to unite previously disparate gender-variant communities around the idea that these groups are all targeted for discrimination because they transgress binary gender norms. Activists such as Kate Bornstein, Leslie Feinberg, Riki Wilchins and countless others mobilized many transgender spectrum folks, and won over many feminist and queer allies, by positioning the transgender community as the cutting edge of a much broader movement to shatter the gender binary. In 1999, Wilchins and other transgender activists took this approach to MWMF, where they revived Camp Trans (after a five-year hiatus) and challenged the "womyn-born-womyn"-only policy on the basis that it is rooted in outdated, binary assumptions about gender.

The idea that transgender identities and expression subvert the gender binary did much to increase transgender-inclusion within feminist and queer spaces. However, this approach did not benefit all transgender people equally. Because transgender-inclusion was explicitly linked to gender transgression and subverting the gender binary, those individuals who did not identify within the gender binary—for example, people who are genderqueer, gender-fluid, or who engage in "genderfuck" (purposefully playing or screwing with gender expression and presentation)—tended to be most celebrated, whereas transsexuals—especially those who identify within the binary and who appear gender-normative and/ or heterosexual post-transition—frequently still had their motives and identities questioned.

It is also common for trans feminine spectrum individuals to be called out for "reinforcing the gender binary" more so than their counterparts on the trans masculine spectrum. This is due, in part, to the fact that female and feminine appearances are more readily and routinely judged in our society than male and masculine ones. And because concepts like "transgression" and "rebellion" tend to be coded as "masculine" in our culture, whereas "conformity" and "conventionality" are typically coded as "feminine," there is an unspoken bias that leads masculine transgender expression to be seen as more inherently transgressive than feminine transgender expression. Indeed, such unconscious presumptions about masculinity and femininity have surely contributed to the tendency exhibited by many feminists to praise women who engage in traditionally "masculine" endeavors, while expressing anywhere from apathy to antagonism toward men who engage in traditionally "feminine" endeavors. In fact, one could make the case that historically feminism has been predisposed toward "trans-masculinism"—that is, favoring gender transgression in the masculine direction.

Not coincidently, perhaps the biggest change in lesbian and queer women's communities since the rise of queer theory and transgender activism has been a growing influx of trans men and others on the trans masculine spectrum, many of whom date and/ or are partnered to non-trans queer women. While trans men are not officially allowed in MWMF, many still attend anyway (as the festival has essentially had a "don't ask, don't tell" policy regarding gender identity for much of the last decade). The significant attendance of trans male/masculine folks led one trans masculine attendee in 2000 to remark that the festival was "the largest female-to-male trans conference I have ever seen in my life." The festival not only accommodates such individuals, but has invited trans masculine musical artists who go by the pronoun "he" to perform on the festival stage. It has also become increasingly common for MWMF supporters to claim that the festival is a place for those who have grown up female in a patriarchal society, an interpretation that conveniently enables trans men to attend but not trans women. Indeed, this growing inclusion of trans men has not yielded a similar inclusion of trans women; in fact, many feel that it has only served to make trans women more invisible and irrelevant within queer women's communities.

Trans-Misogyny, Intersectionality and "Second Wave" Transgender Activism

I personally became involved in the MWMF trans woman-exclusion issue in 2003 when I attended Camp Trans. This was a turning-point year for the protest, as organizers began to make a purposeful effort to focus specifically on working toward trans woman-inclusion (rather than "transgender-inclusion" more generally) and to try to shift the dynamics of the protest from one that favored trans men and others on the trans masculine spectrum to one that is equally welcoming of, and empowering for, trans women. It was there that I first had in-depth conversations with other trans women about how people on the trans feminine spectrum tend to be more routinely derided and demonized— both in mainstream society and within lesbian and queer women's spaces like MWMF—than our trans masculine counterparts. It was clear to many of us that this phenomenon was not simply the result of the fact that we "transgress gender norms" (something both trans masculine and trans feminine folks do). Rather, it seemed to be driven more by traditional sexism—that is, the presumption that femaleness and femininity are inferior to, or less legitimate than, maleness and masculinity.

Over the last five years, trans feminine feminists have begun to articulate a new perspective on feminism and trans activism that better captures our own experiences dealing with sexism. This approach is not so much rooted in queer theory as it is in intersectionality—a theory that grew out of the work of feminists of color, most thoroughly chronicled by Patricia Hill Collins, and perhaps first discussed in relation to the MWMF trans woman-exclusion issue by Emi Koyama. Intersectionality states that different forms of oppression do not act independently of one another, but rather they interact synergistically. Unlike queer theory and lesbian-feminism, intersectionality focuses primarily on the ways in which people are institutionally marginalized, rather than fixating on whether any given individual's identity or behaviors "reinforce" or "subvert" the gender system.

According to this view, trans women lie at the intersection of (at least) two types of sexism. The first is cissexism, which is the societal-wide tendency to view transsexual gender identities and sex embodiments as being less legitimate than those of cissexuals —that is, nontranssexuals. (Note: the word "cisgender" is similarly used as a synonym for nontransgender.) Cissexism functions in a manner analogous to heterosexism: Transsexual gender identities and homosexual/bisexual orientations are both typically viewed as being inherently questionable, unnatural, morally suspect, and less socially and legally valid than their cissexual and heterosexual counterparts. Not only does cissexism institutionally marginalize transsexual individuals, but it privileges cissexuals, rendering their genders and sexed bodies as unquestionable, unmarked and taken for granted (similar to how heterosexual attraction and relationships are privileged in our culture).

While all transsexuals face cissexism, trans women experience this form of sexism as being especially exacerbated by traditional sexism. For example, trans women are routinely hyper-sexualized in our society, especially in the media, where we are regularly depicted as fetishists, sexual deceivers, sex workers and/or in a sexually provocative fashion (trans men, in contrast, are not typically depicted in this way). The common presumption that trans women transition to female for sexual reasons seems to be based on the premise that women as a whole have no worth beyond their ability to be sexualized. Furthermore, most of the societal consternation, ridicule and violence directed at trans people focuses on individuals on the trans feminine spectrum—often specifically targeting our desire to be female or our feminine presentation. While trans men experience cissexism, their desire to be male/masculine is typically not mocked or derided in the same way—to do so would bring maleness/masculinity itself into question. Thus, those of us on the trans feminine spectrum don't merely experience cissexism or "transphobia" so much as we experience trans-misogyny.

Trans feminine perspectives on sexism have shaken up the dynamics of long-standing feminist debates about trans individuals and inclusion. For example, lesbian-feminist critiques of queer theory and transgender activism have charged that focusing primarily on transgressing or blurring the distinction between "woman" and "man" does nothing to address the affect that traditional sexism has on women's lives. Trans feminine feminists typically agree with this lesbian-feminist critique and further extend it to address the many ways in which traditional sexism impacts our own lives, both as women and as trans women.

Trans feminine feminists have also taken issue with the ways in which others have defined and positioned us in the MWMF inclusion debate. For example, queer theorists and transgender activists often argue for inclusion on the basis that transgender people transgress or subvert the gender binary. Trans women have challenged this approach for being both masculine-centric (as it favors trans masculine individuals) and cissexist (as the presumption that we blur or subvert the gender binary is the direct result of people viewing us as "fake" and "illegitimate" women in the first place). Lesbian-feminists, on the other hand, typically argue that trans women should be denied entrance into women-only spaces such as MWMF because we were born and socialized male. These claims are also masculine-centric (as they emphasize supposedly "male/masculine" aspects of our history over our female identities and lived experiences as women) and cissexist (as they presume that our female identities are less legitimate than those of cissexual women).

Trans feminine feminists have also countered the way in which MWMF has increasingly co-opted queer/transgender rhetoric in recent years in its defense of its trans woman-exclusion policy. For example, a 2006 MWMF press release described "womyn-born-womyn" as "a valid and honorable gender identity." This statement seems to takes advantage of the transgender activist claim that there are countless possible gender identities, each of which should be equally respected. However, it fails to recognize who the privileged majority is in this case (cissexual women/"womyn-born-womyn") and who the marginalized minority is (transsexual women). Thus, MWMF's statement is analogous to the hypothetical situation of heterosexual women declaring that "straight woman" is a valid gender identity in order to justify excluding lesbian and bisexual women from an event in which all other women are welcome. Most MWMF supporters would undoubtedly recognize such an approach as being unquestionably heterosexist; by the same reasoning, MWMF's trans woman-exclusion policy is unquestionably cissexist. MWMF has also asserted that the festival is not "transphobic" because plenty of transgender people attend, or because it is "home to womyn who could be considered gender outlaws" (an apparent reference to Kate Bornstein's binary-shattering book Gender Outlaw: On Men, Women and the Rest of Us). While this strategy gives the appearance of accommodating queer/transgender perspectives, it does not address the concerns of trans feminine feminists, who believe that the festival's policy is primarily cissexist and trans-misogynistic/trans-masculinist (as it is excludes trans women while accommodating trans male/masculine folks).

A recognition of trans-misogyny/trans-masculinism—both within queer and feminist settings, and in society at large—has led many trans women and trans male allies to critique the growing numbers of trans men who, despite their physical transitions and the fact that they now live as men, still feel entitled to inhabit lesbian and women's spaces. Such individuals will often justify their continued presence in such spaces by citing their female history, or claiming that they don't feel 100 percent like a "man" (even though their appearance definitely reads "man"). Such claims reinforce the popular misconception that transsexual gender identities should not be taken seriously, and thus has had a direct negative impact on trans women's inclusion in these same spaces. In a sense, these trans men seem to want to have it both ways: being men in the male-centered mainstream and then being "not-men" in queer/women's/feminist spaces. This places trans women in no-win situation: We are treated as second-class citizens in the male-centered mainstream because we are women, and then further derided for supposedly being privileged, infiltrating "men" in queer/feminist/women's spaces.

This growing "gender gap" between trans masculine and trans feminine communities is not unique to the MWMF trans woman-exclusion debate, but can be seen in other areas of transgender activism. While trans men used to be a minority in the trans community, over the last 15 years their numbers have significantly increased and, in many cities and college campuses, they have come to dominate transgender organizations and activism. This prominence is often enabled by the trans-masculinist leanings of feminist and queer activism (which tend to be suspicious of, or less welcoming toward, trans women both before and after our transitions). Trans men also enjoy significant social advantages over trans women, both because they physically tend to "pass" as cissexuals more often and more easily than trans women, and because of the male privilege they experience post-transition. Trans women—especially those who transition at a young age and who thus do not benefit significantly from male privilege pre-transition—have more difficulties finding and maintaining employment, are more susceptible to poverty, and are more likely to engage in survival sex work to make ends meet. There is a growing sense among many trans women that previous models of transgender activism have largely ignored these trans female/ feminine-specific issues in a manner similar to how progressive movements during the 1960s largely ignored woman-specific issues, and how the gay rights movement of the 1970s and 1980s largely ignored lesbian-specific issues.

Trans feminine feminists are not the only group critiquing the "first wave" of transgender activism for ignoring the ways in which transgender issues are often intertwined with, and exacerbated by, other forms of oppression. Since the early 2000s, a number of organizations—such as the Sylvia Rivera Law Project, TransJustice, Trans/Gender Variant in Prison and others—have begun to focus specifically on the needs of trans people of color, trans people of low income, and those who are incarcerated—all of whom are especially vulnerable to gender regulation and oppression due to living at the intersection of racism, classism and sexism. As a testament to the importance of intersectionality, a GenderPAC report on violence against gender non-conforming youth showed that the vast majority of the victims were of color, poor or on the trans feminine spectrum (and very often, all three). Activists like Viviane Namaste and Mirha-Soleil Ross have pointed out that trans sex workers—typically poor trans women and trans feminine spectrum individuals—receive little to no attention or support from mainstream transgender organizations, activists and academics, despite the fact that they are arguably the most marginalized segment of the transgender community. Other activists, such as Monica Roberts—who blogs under the name TransGriot and who is one of the organizers of the annual Transsistahs and Transbrothas Conference—have written extensively about how mainstream transgender organizations routinely fail to acknowledge issues that disproportionately affect trans people of color. Just as universalizing views of womanhood that existed within "second wave" feminism were challenged by "third wave" feminists, the universalizing view of transgender people forwarded in the 1990s (which tended to ignore differences with regard to race, class and direction of transition and/or transgender expression) have increasingly been called into question by this "second wave" of transgender activism.

Given the violence and extreme poverty that afflicts many trans people, some have suggested that the MWMF trans woman-exclusion issue has received an undeserved amount of activist attention. And the fact that tickets to this weeklong festival cost several hundred dollars—a luxury many trans folks cannot afford —is often cited by those who view MWMF's policy as primarily a middle-class trans issue. While MWMF is not the most pressing trans-related issue out there, such critiques miss the larger picture. This is not about the desire to simply attend one music festival. Rather, for lesbian and bisexual trans women, this is about us being able to participate in our own queer women's community —a community in which we face anywhere from antagonism to irrelevancy on a regular basis.

Perhaps more importantly, this is about us being able to have a voice within feminism more generally. MWMF is not only the world's largest annual women-only event, but historically it's been a focal point for dialogues and debates on a wide range of feminist issues. As someone who has experienced firsthand the substantial difference between what it's like to be treated as a woman and as a man, and who now experiences both misogyny and trans-misogyny in my day-to-day life, I have found feminism to be an indispensable foundation for me to make sense of my experiences and to articulate the obstacles and issues that I face. For many of us who are trans women, this is about having a voice in a movement that is incommensurably vital to us.

For years, trans women have effectively had no voice in MWMF. During that time, many cissexual women and trans masculine attendees have tried to advocate on our behalf inside the festival. While their intensions may have been sincere, the fact that they entered into a space that excludes trans women, and that they claimed to speak for us (despite not having had a trans female/feminine life experience themselves), their actions further contributed to the erasure of our voices and perspectives. While the "womyn-born-womyn"-only policy remains in effect to this day, MWMF stopped formally expelling trans women from the festival in 2006 (although they still insist that any trans woman who attends is "choosing to disrespect the stated intention of this festival").

While the situation is hardly perfect, it does for the first time allow trans women to speak in their own voices within MWMF. And that's a crucial part of any feminist or activist movement: to allow those who have been marginalized, disenfranchised and excluded to be able to define themselves, and to speak in their own voices about the struggles they face and the way they experience their own lives.

> "*[The editors] want not just to show that we are everywhere, but to show how that "we" is constructed, and who is left out."*

Intersectionality Can Be Left Out of Identity Politics

Hugh Ryan

In the following viewpoint, author Hugh Ryan examines how the identity of "queerness" is often seen as being the domain of city dwellers and far removed from rural parts of the country. Reviewing a new anthology entitled Queering the Countryside, *Ryan works to excavate how queer became a political identity associated with middle- and upper-class urbanites. He asks, "What would it mean for the poor and rural queer to become incorporated into the queer movement and to be considered in a positive light?" This question is at the heart of not only what identity politics encompasses, but who and what it excludes. Ryan is a journalist, curator, and speaker whose work has appeared in the* New York Times, *the* Guardian, VICE, *and Slate.*

"Queer in Rural America," by Hugh Ryan, October 18, 2016. Reprinted by permission.

As you read, consider the following questions:

1. Why is queerness associated with certain "gayborhoods?"
2. What is the importance of holding LGBTQ summits in rural areas?
3. Why does the author focus on "rurality and queerness?" How does this focus on location and identity shift the conversation on identity politics?

The queer rights movement has created a plethora of memorable slogans: *Silence = Death, Gay Is Good, Out of the Closets and into the Streets.* But my favorite is the deceptively mild *We Are Everywhere.* To homophobes, it evokes horror-movie tropes, half *Invasion of the Body Snatchers,* half "the call is coming from inside the house." To queer people, however, it whispers of a community hidden in plain sight, of queerness bursting forth unexpectedly like water from the rock at Rephidim. The political plasticity of "we" makes it the perfect basis for queer organizing, as it evokes a sexuality that is expressed not via particular actions or identities, but solely through solidarity with other queers—yet therein also lies a problem. If the foundation of our organizing requires placing a premium on our sexuality or gender identity as it has been defined by a largely white, urban, bourgeois queer movement, what happens to same-sex loving, gender non-conforming individuals who can't, don't, or won't fit the mold? Are they less queer, or simply less considered? As neighborhoods, nonprofits, and social-justice movements get built by and for those whose primary identification is around a particular vision of queerness, it becomes harder and harder to see the needs, ideas, or very existence of other queers. And because this kind of organization *requires* aggregation, it tends to happen in cities and lionize urban life, whose sexual skyscrapers cast long, obscuring shadows over the towns and fields of rural queerness.

Indeed many see queer sexuality as inseparable from famous gayborhoods such as New York City's Greenwich Village, San

Francisco's Castro, and Chicago's Boystown. In the biomythography of many American queers, the countryside is the place we escape from, the grim before to our urban happily-ever-after. However, this stereotype obscures the fact that many queer Americans, either by chance or by choice, dwell in small towns and rural places. Overlooked by the national gay rights movement and underrepresented in the media, they have rarely been seen as important subjects for scholarship and political representation. And when they are, it is often after some tragedy, such as the murders of Brandon Teena and Matthew Shepard.

For many gay Americans, the countryside is a place we escaped. But what would it mean to consider rural queerness in a positive light?

A new anthology, *Queering the Countryside*, joins a growing body of literature that seeks to offer a corrective to this metro-chauvinism, turning attention to the daily lives of queer rural Americans. In their introduction, the editors emphasize that "'rural America' in neither a monolith nor an apparition." In particular, they seek to pivot away from the popular sentiments that "rural" always connotes whiteness, conservatism, or cisgender identity; that rural spaces in America are only important in the past, not the present; and that the only healthy, happy way to be gay today is as an out urbanite.

Perhaps it is not surprising, given these lofty ambitions, that *Queering the Countryside* often falls short, particularly in conveying a rich sense of life as a rural queer person. Too frequently the book emphasizes the conceptual over the actual, the detritus of sexuality over the experience of it, the "theory" over the "queer." When queer people do appear, they often feel like raw material waiting for a benevolent academic to spin the dross of their lives into golden theory. Largely absent are the lived nuances evocatively captured in recent journalism on, for example, gay and lesbian organic farmers, queer rural communes, and even queer sauerkraut production. One is instead left with a sense of rural queerness that is predominantly inhabited, contrary to the editors' ambitions, by white, cisgender people. This is hardly surprising, since race and gender identity are two of the shoals that queer thinking has traditionally foundered on, particularly in projects that are not organized by people of color or trans people themselves.

One of the points that *Queering the Countryside* makes eloquently is that rural queer people tend to emphasize local connections and community as much as, or more than, the intentional communities of far-flung queerness. They may therefore have little that obviously distinguishes them from their neighbors. Many may not wish to be found—a challenge with which *Queering the Countryside* struggles. One of the most obvious results was a stretching of what constitutes "rural." For example, one of the volume's essays focuses on Asheville, North Carolina—a city that by the book's own definition is not rural. The editors of *Queering the Countryside* adopt the U.S. Census Bureau's definition of urban clusters as "cities with populations of at least fifty thousand." With 87,000 people, Asheville stands well above this threshold. This elision of "Southern" with "rural" highlights how capacious our notions of rural spaces are, and how even experts can be guilty of the romantic tendency to shoehorn whole regions of America into bucolic notions of "the countryside." As this is one of the few articles that focuses on people of color, this stretching seems intended to diversify the volume, but it is a pyrrhic victory: the book seems more diverse, but "the country" itself is left feeling whiter.

Another essay in the volume, Carly Thomsen's "In Plain(s) Sight: Rural LGBTQ Women and the Politics of Visibility," attempts to navigate the intersectional realities of rural queer people of color. Focused on the 2009 dismissal of Air Force sergeant Jene Newsome, it insightfully teases out the tensions between how rural and urban queers situate sexuality within their public identities. Newsome, a black lesbian from rural Pennsylvania stationed in Rapid City, South Dakota, was dismissed from service after military police learned about her marriage to another woman. In the ensuing legal battle, Newsome and her local supporters focused almost entirely on the issue of *how* the military discovered her marriage—through information illegally passed on by local police—while national LGBT and civil rights organizations dwelled on same-sex marriage rights and the constitutionality of "Don't Ask, Don't Tell."

In her analysis, Thomsen argues that Newsome's strategy relied on rural values of privacy and protecting your fellow community members, whereas an explicit focus on LGBTQ rights would have required her to differentiate herself from her neighbors. Thomsen persuasively argues that the gay rights movement's emphasis on identity politics puts rural queers in a difficult—at times untenable—position. She also articulates a critical point about the limitations of a queer politics of visibility, which so often runs roughshod over nuanced matters of intersectionality. Thomson notes, for example, that the media and national LGBTQ organizations, in focusing on Newsome's lesbianism, problematically avoided any discussion of the role race may have played in the ease of her dismissal, as though drawing attention to this factor would uncouple her from notions of Midwestern wholesomeness and make her a less sympathetic plaintiff. This strategy rendered Newsome's race unspeakable and reinforced the stereotype that rural America is, by definition, a white space.

There is a faux-truism in America that LGBT folks do not fare well in the countryside. This is continually reinforced by the media, who only talk about rural queerness in the context of high-profile murders or low-life government officials. Like many of the videos in Dan Savage's "It Gets Better" project, this suggests that the route to happiness for gay folks leads inexorably away from the countryside. *Queering the Countryside* seeks to correct this perception, but focuses too strongly on the rural past and what is difficult in modern queer rural life. Without a compensatory focus on what is generative or beautiful, this reinforces the stereotype that queerness and rurality are incompatible.

What would it mean to consider rural queerness in a positive light? A good starting point is to examine actual rural queer organizations and queer rural utopian collectives. (I term them this way to draw attention to the fact that the first emerges from the rural experience and looks toward queerness, while the second is rooted in queerness and dreaming of the countryside.)

In recent years there has been an explosion in rural queer organizing. In August Drake University Law School in Des Moines hosted the Iowa Rural LGBT Summit, the fifteenth such rural queer summit organized by the United States Department of Agriculture *in the last two years*. Topics of presentations ranged from microloans as a way to support queer rural people to the creation of supportive senior housing and the need for resources for queer migrant farm workers.

Outside of the academic world of university conferences, grassroots organizing is being done by groups such as Southerners on New Ground, a decades-old social justice organization that "envision[s] a multi-issue southern justice movement . . . in which LGBTQ people—poor and working class, immigrant, people of color, rural—take our rightful place as leaders shaping our region's legacy and future." Newer projects, such as Rachel Garringer's Country Queers oral history archive and the film *Forbidden: Undocumented and Queer in Rural America*, seek to document the lives of rural queer people in their own words. YouTube is also fast becoming its own archive and networking tool for rural queers, providing a place to discuss everything from coming out in rural Virginia, to returning to the Navajo reservation in Crownpoint, New Mexico, to Arkansas's rural gay radio broadcasts of the 1990s. Paralleling this development, rural projects aimed at general audiences have begun to include queer content, such as the "LGBT In Appalachia" panel series at the 2014 Appalachian Studies Association conference. Such mainstreamed initiatives may ultimately have the greatest success reaching rural queer people, many of whom are unlikely to seek out specifically queer resources and networks.

These projects organize outward from the lived experiences of rural queers. Queer rural utopian projects, on the other hand, take as their starting point a rejection of urbanism—which may or may not be based on actual rural experience. They posit "the rural" as a panacea for the perceived problems of modernity, queer or otherwise: lack of community, loneliness, deracination, environmental devastation, disenchantment. Like similar religious communities in early America, many of these groups are to some degree millenarian, preparing an idyllic and self-reliant life in preparation for an inevitable and fast-approaching apocalypse. Many seek to create queer rural oases that reject dominant American social and sexual structures.

In their early days, these queer rural utopian groups were often, and perhaps ironically, gender-essentializing, with lesbians creating wymyn's land collectives around the country, and gay men flocking to "faggot-only" Radical Faerie gatherings organized by communist luminary Harry Hay. The degree to which transfolk were welcome in these spaces varied from group to group, as was true for people of color as well—much like in the rest of the organized, mainstream lesbian and gay movements of the era. But though the countryside is often derided as a place where change comes slowly or not at all, queer rural utopianism has rapidly evolved from these roots. Today collectives such as Sojourners Land celebrate "Black Queer and Transgender Women," while a recent issue of the Radical Faerie Digest explored queer radical utopianism through the perspective of queers with disabilities. Although the popularity of such projects is hard to quantify, a quick search for the word "queer" in the directory of the Fellowship for Intentional Community brings up a whole host of other communes created by or embracing of queers.

The final chapter of *Queering the Countryside* touches on queer rural utopianism, but does so by foregrounding theoretical interests in "queer temporality" and how queer rural communes express "the materiality of time." The result prizes speculation *about* queer rural people over insight *from* them, creating a sense of distance and superiority. Actual queer rural people seem always somehow outside the grasp of *Queering the Countryside*. In their introduction, the editors are rightly critical of gauzy, hagiographic projects that content themselves with "proving that same-sex sexual behavior and gender nonconformity happens" in rural places. Their frame is bigger, their goals nobler. They want not just to show that we are everywhere, but to show how that "we" is constructed, and who is left out. But from such a great height, the countryside and its people blend into familiarly indistinct fields.

> "*Mainstream liberals in America also don't really challenge white privilege. As a consequence white privilege is conceived as a conspiracy theory of the left.*"

White Privilege Has Led to a Stronger Alt-Right Movement

Maria Murriel

In the following viewpoint, Maria Murriel examines the alt-right movement to see how they see themselves. Starting with well-known figures in the alt-right movement such as Milo Yiannopoulos, Murriel explores the different groups of white nationalists and their denial about the way in which their beliefs are rooted in racism. Richard Spencer, who has claimed that he began the alt-right movement, for example, states that he is not racist while also stating that he does not believe that all races are equal. Murriel argues that this denial is rooted in what she calls white privilege, which she defines as being complacent to racism or engaging in racism while denying that it is rooted in racist beliefs. Murriel is a reporter and editor for Public Radio International.

"The 'Alt-Right' and White Outrage Around the World: An Explainer," by Maria Murriel, Public Radio International, November 25, 2016. Reprinted by permission.

As you read, consider the following questions:

1. What are the differences between the groups mentioned in this viewpoint?
2. Why does professor Cas Mudde suggest that the rise of the alt-right is caused by a failing by mainstream liberals?
3. What is "white privilege"?

Journalists and social media users apply the label, short for "alternative right," to a broad range of people. Too broad, according to University of Georgia professor Cas Mudde.

"I don't particularly like the term, because...in its current use, it goes from pretty much neo-Nazis to conservatives," Mudde says. "And on top of that, because it is so broad, it is normalizing white supremacist [thinking]."

Mudde's analysis of this movement is the same as the Anti-Defamation League's: the so-called alt-right are people who "reject mainstream conservatism in favor of forms of conservatism that embrace implicit or explicit racism or white supremacy."

But how does the alt-right see itself?

A New Brand of White Supremacists Who Deny That's What They Are

White nationalist Richard Spencer claims the term alt-right as his creation. He heads the National Policy Institute, which is described as "an independent organization dedicated to the heritage, identity, and future of people of European descent in the United States, and around the world."

Spencer does have specific white nationalist ideals—chiefly, the dream of a white ethno-state—and says everyone in the movement either agrees with him or will at some point.

But in practice the term "alt-right" has come to encompass a mishmash of people.

Breitbart poster-troll Milo Yiannopoulos says he doesn't consider himself a member of the alt-right, though he often speaks and writes about it. He co-authored an explainer about the movement on Breitbart's far-right website: "An Establishment Conservative's Guide to the Alt-Right." It's well worth a read. The piece breaks down the alt-right population into categories (such as "the intellectuals," "the meme team," "natural conservatives"), and combats accusations that the movement is purely based on racism.

The Breitbart piece classifies one type of alt-righter, the "1488er," as a member of the movement's truly racist faction, which it contends is small. "1488" is a neo-Nazi code to referring to the slogan "We Must Secure The Existence Of Our People And A Future For White Children" and "Heil Hitler." These are neo-Nazis.

But the largest swath of the alt-right, the Breitbart story says, are "natural conservatives" who are "mostly white, mostly male middle-American radicals, who are unapologetically embracing a new identity politics that prioritises the interests of their own demographic." These are white supremacists.

Spencer contends "white supremacist" is an offensive term and not at all what his movement is about.

"A white supremacist is someone who wants to rule over other races. You want to be supreme above them," he says. "That is not what I want and it's not what anyone in the alt-right wants."

Yet the words Spencer uses to describe his own views express a clear belief in white superiority.

At his NPI conference in Washington, DC last weekend, Spencer told the crowd white people are a "race of conquerors," and the United States is their "inheritance." (In an interview with The World, Spencer attributed his tone … to the crowd being in a "celebratory mood.")

After the NPI conference, Spencer appeared on TV One, where he remarked on the "genius" of white Europeans, and said that "white people don't ultimately need other races in order to succeed."

"I think that white people, Europeans, formed the core of American identity," he told Roland Martin. Later, he stated plainly: "I do not believe that everyone's equal."

"So you don't believe in multi-racial equality?" Martin asked.

"No. I don't think anyone does actually," Spencer answered.

Yiannopolous also contends that white supremacy is not what the alt-right's all about. At a talk in Houston, he said, "the left is obsessed by white supremacy, which in reality makes up an infinitesimally small number of people."

And he explained what he thought were the true catalysts for alt-right ideology.

"The first is a millennial generation that's fed up with identity politics and its hypocrisies," he said. Being outside the political establishment is a unifying feeling for the alt-right, and presumably what its members would prefer media coverage to focus on—politically disenfranchised youth and their converted elders.

"The second is anti-white racism," he continued. "Ironically so-called white privilege is the privilege to be discriminated against."

Blindness to Privilege

Although most Americans who voted for Donald Trump may not consider themselves part of the alt-right movement, the University of Georgia's Mudde says they could still be aligned with the thinking.

"What this comes down to is not ideological racism," Mudde says. "This is about white Christian male privilege, and the problem with privilege is that you don't see that it is privilege."

This election, 72 percent of white men without college degrees voted for Trump. Fifty-eight percent of Trump voters were classified as "Protestant or other Christian."

Spencer told the BBC in September that he cares about "my people [whites] more than other people," and that he wants to "expand white privilege and deepen it." In an interview with Reveal's Al Letson, he added his belief that "we live in a world of a white-guilt complex."

Mudde says people who benefit from white, male, Christian privilege "don't understand that some of the things that they have, they have because of privilege."

And that's partly the fault of liberals, he adds.

A Ban on Identity Politics in India

On Monday, India's Supreme Court ruled that candidates for political office cannot appeal to voters on the basis of religion, caste, community, or language. The Court maintained that India is a secular country, and these categories are therefore irrelevant to the political process.

The ruling stated, "Religion has no role in electoral process, which is a secular activity. Mixing state with religion is not constitutionally permissible."

The statement sounds like a step toward a balanced political system, an effort to provide a more equal opportunity for able candidates without strong support from a particular religious community.

However, that rule may prove to be minimally practical in a country where religious and community identity is the strongest political factor for a significant portion of the population.

India is home to a dizzying variety of ethnic and religious identities. There are six major religions listed on the Indian census, plus over seven million people who do not practice one of those six religious. There are 14 official languages with hundreds of dialects, and even Hindi, which is the most prominent language, is not spoken by a majority. There are 35 states and thousands of ethnic and tribal groups.

Political leaders have not expressed much faith in this resolution. "If this judgment is taken literally, then pretty much every single party in India could be disqualified," said Ashok Malik, a fellow at the Delhi-based Observer Research Foundation.

On occasion, identity-based politics are a tool for good in India. For instance, the Indian parliament maintains quotas for underrepresented groups like Muslims, who are only 13.4 percent of the population. Studies have shown that better Muslim representation in government "leads to large and significant improvements in child survival rates and improvements in educational attainment." The Dalit, or Untouchable, caste is also allotted a quota of 84 seats in the national parliament.

The *Times of India* claimed that "identity-based political movements as exemplified by the Dalit-centric BSP or the Tamil-based DMK aren't negative in themselves. In fact, these political movements have helped sections of society that have felt marginalized highlight their grievances."

"India Bans Identity Politics In Political Campaigns," by Erin Rubin, Nonprofit Quarterly, January 5, 2017.

"Mainstream liberals in America also don't really challenge white privilege," Mudde says. "As a consequence white privilege is conceived as a conspiracy theory of the left."

"Anti-white Racism" Around the World

Mudde, who hails from the Netherlands and is also the author of "The Populist Radical Right: A Reader," says this feeling that whites are suffering "anti-white racism" is no new thing.

"That has been going on for, like, three decades in Europe," he says. "The redefinition of who is the real victim; the argument is that political correctness has ruined everything, that minorities get everything and if white people speak out about it they're hit with political correctness."

Indeed, that idea has flowed plenty in the US conservative mainstream. The problem of political correctness was a theme at the Republican National Convention in Cleveland this summer. It has been a talking point on Fox News for years.

Spencer draws inspiration from European identitarians, whom the Southern Poverty Law Center says "want regions and nations that are different from one another—but at the same time culturally and ethnically homogeneous within their borders."

But Mudde says "identitarian" doesn't equal "alt-right," as much as the US movement may try to connect itself to the brand.

Boiled down, Mudde explains identitarian thinking as the idea that people do better in their own countries—a German in Germany and an Italian in Italy—but says identitarians also believe in an overarching European identity. So, an Italian in Germany would fare better than a Syrian in Germany would.

"[Identitarians] don't have the same outright anti-Semitism and racial views [as the alt-right]," Mudde says. "They're white supremacists, most of the people we call the alt-right."

Spencer thinks Mudde is making the wrong distinctions.

"[Mudde] is basically trying to hold on to ethnoculture," he says. "And he's trying to take race out of it. And I don't think you can."

As an example, Spencer suggested that he has more in common with a white Australian than with a non-white Italian—in other words, that race is a more powerful identifier than ethnicity.

Andrew Marantz has been writing about the alt-right for the New Yorker, and points out that there are people in the movement who might not subscribe to every idea.

"[But] there are some who are openly white nationalist," he says, "who are interested in preserving European power and European-American power." That is Spencer's NPI mission statement—for people of European descent to prevail around the world.

Marantz says the movement in the US has been networking with similar groups in Europe—in the UK, the Netherlands and France.

Each country's white movement is different, he says, but there are commonalities: "A common thread is what they would call 'secure borders' and what a lot of people would call 'extreme nationalism'...shutting down immigration, deporting people who are already in your country, painting immigrants as a violent threat."

These are also the areas where white movements' causes tend to merge with politics. The tweet below is by anti-Islam Dutch populist Geert Wilders, a political party leader who is facing charges of hate speech. He has lauded Trump on multiple occasions.

Is This Really So Alarming?

Mudde emphasizes that these movements have existed for a long time. He doesn't think they're necessarily more powerful or influential today.

"There's always been an international network of white supremacists," he says, "but those are really, really marginal groups. Mostly neo-Nazi groups. And they stilll exist, but there hasn›t been a clear rise in them."

And even with the appointment of Breitbart's Stephen Bannon as Trump's chief strategist, Mudde's not convinced the so-called alt-right is sure to influence the White House.

But Lawrence Rosenthal of the Center for Right Wing Studies is certain of it.

"[Bannon] made his bones, as it were, by being kind of the hinge between the racialist alt-right and eventually the mainstream media. He was, in effect, an agent of getting the ideas from the alt-right first into things like Drudge Report, Fox News and then the greater mainstream media. And he was extremely effective at that."

"In general, what the alt-right represents, has been very much at the fringes or at the margins of American politics. Trump has, in effect, institutionalized it. [Bannon is] the first person who presumably Trump turns to say, what's your advice on how I should handle 'blank.'"

"Too often, discussion of religion and atheism in the media centres on personality clashes, or is otherwise presented as a zero-sum game."

We Need a New Approach to Discussing Religion

Daniel Trilling

In the following viewpoint, Daniel Trilling argues that our ways of talking about religion both in the media and outside it have become counterproductive because many of us operate on a flawed set of starting points. In laying out a few basic principles for addressing religion and atheism, the author argues that making assumptions like "Islam is bad because some Muslims do bad things," or "Atheists are smarter than religious people" results in stereotyping and unfair judgments that in turn stifle meaningful discourse. Instead, granting one another respect and opening our minds to a variety of diverse identities are the first steps to understanding each other. Trilling is editor of New Humanist.

As you read, consider the following questions:

1. What global event does the author use as a starting point for a period that was supposed to be more liberal, democratic, and secular?
2. What percentage of England's and Wales's population describe themselves as having no religion?
3. What does the author point out is a major conflict between secularists and believers?

After the fall of the Berlin Wall, we were told that the triumph of capitalism would lead inexorably to the spread of liberal, democratic and secular values. Yet as globalisation has brought down barriers between nation-states, new forms of exclusive, aggressive identity politics have thrived. Sometimes, these are founded on religious belief; other times on culture or ethnicity; others still on twisting the language of tolerance and equal rights so that it can be used to oppress others. One of the most pressing questions of our time is how we negotiate complex ethical and political issues while remaining true to secular values.

Currently, Richard Dawkins is providing a case study in how not to do it. "All the world's Muslims have fewer Nobel Prizes than Trinity College, Cambridge," he tweeted on 8 August, adding: "They did great things in the Middle Ages, though." At first glance a fairly innocuous (if odd) comment, it provoked a storm of condemnation —not only from religious believers, but from many self-declared atheists too. But it's a fact, pleaded Dawkins and his supporters. What's wrong with stating facts? This is disingenuous in the extreme. Dawkins knows full well the importance of context— and as the Independent columnist Owen Jones argued, it was the latest in a long line of statements that have singled out Muslims for particular opprobrium. Jones condemned this in the strongest possible terms as "dressing up bigotry as non-belief," but he wasn't alone. The Telegraph's Tom Chivers, while declaring himself a Dawkins "fan," argued that his rhetoric was not only offensive, but damaging to the atheist cause. Yet Dawkins's response to these criticisms on his blog dismisses the furore that greeted his tweets as a "storm in a teacup" and merely restates previously expressed opinions and shows little willingness to reflect on the valid objections people have raised.

That's his choice. For me, this is about more than Dawkins. Too often, discussion of religion and atheism in the media centres on personality clashes, or is otherwise presented as a zero-sum game. I'll be taking over as editor of *New Humanist* in September, and I want our magazine to stand for something different. This, however, means we must recognise a few basic principles about the way we discuss religion. I've set out three of them below.

Some "Criticism" Of Religion Is Racist

Muslims are not a "race." Nor are the Irish, or Jews, or Pakistanis, nor are the descendants of enslaved plantation workers in the Caribbean—and yet all have been subject to racism within recent history, based on those specific identities. What matters is the political context—and when it comes to discussing Islam, it is foolish to ignore the wider context of Islamophobia, in which religious and cultural differences have been systematically exaggerated to give the impression that Muslims pose a dire threat to the survival of western civilisation. As with anti-Semitism, this not only threatens the devout, but anybody with cultural links to a Muslim community. That doesn't mean there can't be a healthy—and critical—debate about Islam, as there is about other religions. But rhetoric that paints the world's 1.5 billion Muslims as a monolithic bloc, or tries to make out they are uniquely savage, or violent, as a result of their religion, should be cause for alarm.

Religious Believers Are No Less Intelligent Than Non-Believers

The 2011 census revealed 14.1 million people in England and Wales who describe themselves as having "no religion"—a quarter of the population, and a 67 per cent jump since 2001. Does that mean

Britain has become a cleverer place in the last decade? I doubt it. Declaring one's self a non-believer, or an atheist, is not a free pass to the sunlit uplands of truth and reason. And if you regard organised religion as merely a product of misguided beliefs, then you lose the ability to understand why it grows and changes historically, and why politicised forms of religion are so attractive to millions of people around the world. Psychological studies that throw up conclusions like "religious people are less intelligent than atheists" not only rely on an extremely narrow definition of "intelligence," but as their own authors will point out, are influenced by factors such as employment, salary and time spent in the education system.

Secularism Does Not Mean Excluding Religious Believers From Public Life

The great paradox of organised religion is that in offering a better life in the next world, it is making a comment on the inadequacy of the lives we live now. For those of us who don't believe in an afterlife, that gives us no option but to change this world—but we can't do it alone. That's why the key to political progress is an ability to find common ground between people of different religious beliefs and none. It's why we don't want unelected bishops making our laws, but it's also why we don't want laws that stigmatise or discriminate against religious minorities.

What can a magazine like *New Humanist* contribute? We will continue to campaign against the use of blasphemy laws to silence dissenters around the world—and through initiatives like the Apostasy Project, we will work to support those people thinking of leaving religion behind. We will extend our solidarity to those people—atheists and believers alike—who struggle against theocratic regimes, or governments who otherwise manipulate religion in order to maintain power. But above all that, *New Humanist* will be a place for debate, reflection, and new ideas. I hope Richard Dawkins will join us in this—but more importantly, I hope you do, too.

Periodical and Internet Sources Bibliography

The following articles have been selected to supplement the diverse views presented in this chapter.

Tamar W. Carroll, "Intersectionality and Identity Politics: Cross-Identity Coalitions for Progressive Social Change," *Signs*, Spring 2017, http://www.journals.uchicago.edu/doi/full/10.1086/689625.

Kimberlé Crenshaw, "Why Intersectionality Can't Wait," *Washington Post,* September 24, 2015, https://www.washingtonpost.com/news/in-theory/wp/2015/09/24/why-intersectionality-cant-wait.

Michael Darer, "The Recent Spate of Anti 'Identity Politics' Hand-Wringing Is Proof That We Need Intersectionality More Than Ever," *Huffington Post*, December 14, 2016, http://www.huffingtonpost.com/entry/the-recent-spate-of-anti-identity-politics-hand-wringing_us_5851ea52e4b0865ab9d4e910.

Maxine de Havenon, "When Identity Politics Clash with Intersectionality—The Democratic Primary and the 'Women's Vote," *Brown Political Review*, March 14, 2016, http://www.brownpoliticalreview.org/2016/03/when-identity-politics-clashes-with-intersectionality-the-democratic-primary-and-the-womens-vote.

Damon Linker, "Liberals Are Drunk on a Political Poison Called Intersectionality," *Week*, January 11, 2017, http://theweek.com/articles/672265/liberals-are-drunk-political-poison-called-intersectionality.

Ché Ramsden, "'Showing Up': Intersectionality 101," *Open Democracy*, March 21, 2016, https://www.opendemocracy.net/5050/ch-ramsden/showing-up-how-intersectionality-ensures-our-struggles-are-success.

Jaime Utt, "'We're All Just Different!': How Intersectionality is Being Colonized by White People," Thinking Race Blog, April 24, 2017, https://thinkingraceblog.wordpress.com/2017/04/24/were-all-just-different-how-intersectionality-is-being-colonized-by-white-people.

OPPOSING
VIEWPOINTS®
SERIES

CHAPTER 3

How Has Identity Politics Ignored Other Useful Ways of Political Organizing?

Chapter Preface

I dentity politics has often been faced with criticisms from both the liberal left and the conservative right of the political spectrum. However, critiques from the left, and particularly from the Marxist left, often focus on how identity politics leaves out discussion of class. Marxist thought developed from German philosopher and economist Karl Marx's works, including *The Communist Manifesto* and *Das Kapital*. For Marx, class struggle is the building block of societies and the root of all oppression. Many Marxists believe that identity politics is concerned with the symptoms rather than the root of oppression.

Marxists such as Albert Terry, III, whose viewpoint is featured in this chapter, state that those who follow identity politics focus on race and gender to the exclusion of social class. For Terry and others, this is a dangerous omission and has cost the political left many elections.

Other authors featured in this chapter, such as Ramona, agree with Terry on one point: identities are used by states to control populations. However, they disagree on whether or not class struggle is the basis of all oppression or rather one facet of a complicated problem.

Finally, Richard Cravatts focuses not on social class but on free speech. He argues that identity politics has made people unwilling to listen to other perspectives, which has, in turn, eroded free speech. For Cravatts, this is not only oppressive but actually harms liberals' claims to openness and inclusivity and, thus, damages their electoral chances by appearing hypocritical to American voters. This critique comes from the opposite end of the political spectrum to Marxism—conservatism—and has recently found favor among moderates and independents alike.

> *"Identity must be treated not as a political concept, but as a facet of our everyday lives."*

Identity Is Socially Constructed to Maintain State Power

Ramona

In the following viewpoint, Ramona argues that identity politics has its failings. For her, identities are not fixed but are socially constructed. This is important because government and other institutions with power use an idea of fixed identity in order to control populations. The danger of identity politics is that it can form allegiances across classes and encourage radical fighting in the mainstream establishment. For this reason it is important that identity be viewed outside of political power. Ramona identifies as a queer, anarchist communist.

As you read, consider the following questions:

1. What does the author mean when she states that identities are "socially constructed"?
2. What is the "unfortunate connotation" of socially constructed identities?
3. How does the author tie capitalism and economics into her argument?

Introduction

I am a _____ who seeks the destruction of class society. That blank can be filled with a variety of words, from worker to queer to individual to mixed-race person to anarchist. What each of these terms has in common is that they each signify a certain identity. While identity politics have gained traction in both anarchist/radical scenes and society more generally, the very idea of identity politics is a problem. Identity politics, as a political force, seeks inclusion into the ruling classes, rather than acting as a revolutionary force for the destruction of class society. However, this does not mean we should dismiss identity or identity-based organizing and action. The institutions that create and enforce class society (capital, work, the state, police) rely on identities in their strategy of control, by attacking some identities and not others, or by pitting various identities at odds to compete for access to the privilege of acceptance by the dominant classes. In their use of repression based on identities, those in power also create affinity among the dominated. Let this be made clear: I do not contend that every person who identifies with or is identified by a particular social identity has a common experience. Similarly, I do not argue that these identities are anything other than socially constructed. However, I do argue that people who share an identity can find stronger affinity with others who share that identity. This is due to the ways that capitalism and the state enforce identities. While these identities are socially constructed, this does not lessen their importance or their reality. Indeed, it is critical in the struggle for total liberation to understand the ways identities are constructed to subjugate people.

The academics have been speaking for years of "the Other" as the most abstract identity, defined in opposition to the dominant forces. While this abstraction works in the most general comparisons of various identities, it is in the specificities of distinct identities that affinities are built. A discussion of every socially-enforced identity would be impossible; instead, I will focus on an analysis of queer identity. Specifically, I will attempt to articulate an anti-assimilationist and anarchist/communist perspective on queer identity, with implications for other identities as well. This is a perspective critical of identity politics as well as a false unity under any one identity (citizen, human race, proletariat). It is critical of assimilationist politics and practice, and perhaps most importantly, it is explicitly anti-state and anti-capitalist.

Social Construction and Social Facts

To understand identity in the context of the present social order, one must understand the concept of social construction. This concept, in short, refers to the ways in which social institutions establish, regulate, and enforce various identities. One especially telling example is the way in which those labeled "insane" are then forced into institutions which serve only to reaffirm a supposed insanity. Homosexuality was once considered a mental disorder, after all.

The term socially constructed carries an unfortunate connotation, however. It is assumed that if an identity is socially constructed, then it differs in some way from a more authentic, natural identity. This assumption resembles religious dogma in that we are asked to accept an unchanging human nature as defined by someone else. In reality, to say identity is a social construction means that identities are defined and enforced by social institutions such as governments and businesses. Thus, identity becomes social fact in the sense that it materially affects people. From queer-bashing to abortion bans, certain identities carry with them material disadvantages. From property rights to Jim Crow, certain identities carry with them material advantages. These identities are socially constructed, and thus become social facts. These inequalities are not expressions of some preexisting natural order. Instead, the cause of these material inequalities can be traced to the socio-economic context in which they existed. This context is determined by the dominant social order, which continues to be that of capitalism and state power.

Not every act of discrimination or oppression, however, can be considered a direct act of the state or capital. This is particularly true when one considers specific manifestations of patriarchy. Sexual assault and domestic violence are often considered interpersonal disputes, rather than having a larger meaning in the context of a deeply patriarchal social order. However, even if there is not an agent of the state or an agent of capital directly involved, one cannot ignore the social framework which normalizes such behavior. One must only consider the fact that the institution of marriage was originally a property relationship, and even until recent decades rape was acceptable, as long as it was in the context of marriage. This is not to say that perpetrators have any excuse. They still enforce the social system of patriarchy, despite (usually) not acting in an official capacity on behalf of the state or capital.

We can thus trace identity-based oppression to either the official business of state power and capitalism, or else to the power of the statist, capitalist social order. The distinction, however, becomes academic. The problem clearly lies in this society, in the social order and the institutions that create, maintain, and enforce it. Much as identity is social, so is the oppression around it: it is a result of human interactions, not any sort of higher power.

The term social construction means also that identity is not fixed, but rather changes according to a variety of factors. Particularly, there exists a tension between those who benefit from inequality, and those who are oppressed by inequality. In the United States, this tension is demonstrated by the range of identity-liberation movements that have been active in the United States. With a few notable exceptions (women's suffrage being one), identity-movements rose to prominence in the 1960s, as chants of black power, gay is good, and sisterhood is powerful became fixtures at demonstrations and protests. These demonstrations and conflicts were sites of struggle over what was meant when the terms black, gay, or woman were used. To be assigned any of these terms meant that one was not fully human, that there was a defect that nobody could correct. The Black Power, Queer Liberation, and

Women's Liberation movements contested the idea that people were to be defined by these identities and thus undeserving of equality. These contestations (as each movement was, to a large degree, focused only on one specific identity) meant that not only could political inequality be challenged, but also the very definitions of identity. In other words, people began to actively and consciously construct their identities and explore identity in relationship to the larger social structure.

The initial exploration of identity proved useful, providing a greater understanding of the ways in which domination and its specific manifestations (racism, sexism, homophobia) are connected to the state and capitalism. The 1960s were also years of resistance and uprising more generally. These events did not happen separately; instead, they were a part of a larger discontent with society as a whole. However, much as the energy of the 1960s was dissipated into the traditional, rigid forms of activism and managed dissent, so was the revolutionary potential of exploring identity.

Over time, these movements have left us with organizations such as the National Association for the Advancement of Colored People (NAACP), Human Rights Campaign (HRC), and National Organization for Women (NOW) as the self-proclaimed leaders in the struggle for equality under the law. However, what is interesting to note is that these organizations serve as explicitly political organizations, seeking political equality through political processes. These groups can thus be understood to engage in identity politics.

Identity Politics and Anti-Identity Politics

Given the political effectiveness of these organizations, their model has been emulated by others seeking to reform the current socio-economic order. This has led to identity politics becoming a central part of the contemporary United States political order. This is especially true in the liberal reformist movement, where organizations such as the NAACP, HRC, and NOW are prominent. With their successes in political reform, they (and many other identity-politics organizations) have become embedded in the dominant political discourse. It is here that we encounter one of the main problems of identity politics: the groups which sought to challenge identity-based oppression have instead merely entered into a partnership with those who benefit from oppression. This partnership concerns the ability to define the political agenda for a certain identity. This is clearly demonstrated in the queer community by the HRC, with their push for hate crime laws, marriage, and military service. These demands show that the HRC has accepted the logic of and requested partnership in the government and the marketplace. Essentially, the HRC is fighting for assimilation into, rather than the destruction of, a system that creates and enforces the very oppression they are allegedly struggling against.

However, even identity politics does not have unfettered power in the political mainstream. Even the appearance of altering power relations in this society is, to some, a threat. These reactionaries claim that identity politics seeks special rights for certain groups. This flawed logic rests on the idea that, since people are guaranteed equality under the Constitution, then the problem of legal inequality is non-existent. Even if one accepts the logic of the state, the discrepancy between legal/political equality and social equality is telling.

Another reaction to the Left's adoption of identity politics is the rise of hard-Right identity politics. This leads to absurdities such as men's rights movements, white rights movements, and groups dedicated to preserving Christian culture and identity. One can see a connection between these two reactionary positions, despite their apparent contradictions. Each position represents a different tactic towards the same goal: maintaining a class-based society along with the homophobic, white-supremacist, and patriarchal structures that uphold it. This stands in contrast to identity politics, which seeks to mildly reform class society and its institutions.

In short, there today exists a tension between progressive identity politics and reactionary anti-identity politics. The failure of both rests in their reliance on the state and capitalism as basis for their vision of society. Both seek to better manage the present order. It is clear: there exists a subset of people in this society that benefit from the current social order. These people include queer people, people of color, women, and every identity. Politicians, police, prison guards, landlords, and bosses: these are our enemies. They come in all forms.

It is equally clear that queer-bashers, rapists, and racists are similarly enemies of liberation. While in some cases these are not people with access to and the backing of institutional power, the violence they inflict is no less real or important. Indeed, their tactics are taken directly from the state, and uphold systems of control even after the formal powers officially abandon them.

Identity is meaningful in that it marginalizes us in different ways, and the affinity that comes from similar or shared experiences is powerful. However, it must always be remembered that such affinity is rendered useless when it is integrated in a system of domination and control. Such affinity ought to be encouraged, as it strengthens our bonds to one another and promotes conflict with the social order, be it bombing police cars or expelling rapists from one's community.

Identity Anti-Politics: One Mixed-Race Queer's Perspective

A specific sort of affinity is generated between people who are faced with similar oppression based on socially constructed identities. However, problems arise when this affinity is expanded to mean something else, such as an idea of racial unity or gender unity. Affinity cannot be reduced to mere identity: for example, simply because I am mixed-race does not mean I have affinity with all people of color. While we are likely to share similar experiences, merely having such experiences does not constitute affinity. The question of "what constitutes affinity?" is a large one, and well beyond the scope of this work. What is clear, however, is the problem of identity politics to those of us who seek total liberation.

By working within the political arena, identity-politicians work within accepted notions of power, change, and struggle. They become another lobby, another special interest that some politicians are beholden to while others rail against them. The people that constitute these identities are lost in all of this, become a voting bloc to be traded around rather than people. This model fails us. Our lives are not political questions, positions to be taken, or votes to be won. We cannot be reduced into discrete categories of identity, each with its own set of lobbyists to win over the bourgeois politicians. This is the dead-end of assimilationism. This is the dead-end of politics. Rather than more politics, more money for lobbyist, and more ad campaigns, we need an end to the political process.

It is, after all, the politicians who had us criminalized or killed. It is the capitalists who make us work to survive, or sometimes keep us out of work. Why do we petition those who marginalize us for an end to our marginalization? They are interested in expanding their power over us, or at the least maintaining it. It is true that they occasionally allow moderate concessions, but these concessions should not pacify us. These concessions are not liberation, and sometimes they're not even liberating. The expansion of marriage rights? Being allowed to fight in the military? These goals are useless because they are simply political goals; they seek to alter the way the political system functions.

The point is not to achieve equality by the political process. The point is to destroy the political process, and with it the apparatus that props up class society. This requires an anti-political outlook. Identity must be treated not as a political concept, but as a facet of our everyday lives. My experiences have convinced me that the current socio-economic order has to be destroyed. I find stronger affinity with other queer people because of my understanding of homophobia, but I will not vote for gay marriage. I find stronger affinity with other mixed-race people because of my understanding of racism, but I will not vote for harsher hate crime laws.

It is clear that, because identities shape our experiences, we cannot write off identity as unimportant. However, it is equally clear that we cannot afford to maintain the identities imposed upon us. Thus, an apparent contradiction arises between the necessity of recognizing socially constructed identity while simultaneously trying to destroy the class society that enforces those identities. This contradiction proves difficult, with a range of responses from a disregard for the destruction of class society to a disregard for identity, and many other arguments somewhere between these two positions. The problem is that there is no contradiction. Indeed, the former necessitates the latter. In order to destroy class society, an analysis of how it functions is critical. In short, we must know our enemy. However, it is important to avoid the pitfall of essentialism; it must always be understood that these identities are constructed by the larger socio-economic structure. The oppression that affects people with various identities is enforced by state power and the power of capital. Understanding this is generates a premise for solidarity, as those marginalized find affinity within their communities with those who face similar struggles. Additionally, the understanding of connections between one's experience with identity and one's experience with the larger socio-economic order allows for a solidarity that goes beyond any specific identity.

The importance of identity lies not in identity politics, but rather in the fact that identity is socially constructed by the dominant system in order to maintain capitalism and state power. In turn, the oppression that follows is an integral part of the social order as a whole, whether the violence is on an interpersonal, institutional, or structural level. Oppression also helps build affinity, through shared experiences or through shared struggle. Recognizing identity and identity-based oppression as social facts allows for stronger affinity, and the connections between one's experiences and the larger social order similarly allows for a solidarity between people who want to abolish the state, abolish capitalism, and abolish the domination that both maintain over our lives. This abolition requires not political negotiation, but anti-political organizing and action.

> "[The] drive for identity recognition is perhaps the most distinctly modern political movement."

Identity Politics Is an Important Modern Political Movement

Jason Blakely

In the following viewpoint, Jason Blakely argues that identity politics is not a failed experiment but that we should work to understand the role it plays in our society and how societies can focus less on individual identity and more on pluralism in governance. In the wake of Donald Trump's surprising victory in the 2016 US presidential election, many commentators spoke out about the "failings" of identity politics and its usurpation by an ultra-right, nationalist group. Blakely is an assistant professor of political science at Pepperdine University. He writes on politics, philosophy, and human behavior.

As you read, consider the following questions:

1. What does the author identify as one of the most jarring revelations of the 2016 presidential election?
2. What is the specific anxiety that modern people are afflicted with, according to the author?
3. What steps is Charles Taylor quoted as suggesting when engaging with political opponents?

"Learning to Live With Identity Politics In the Age of Trump," by Jason Blakely, America Press Inc., January 20, 2017. Reprinted by permission.

C hris Arnade, a tireless chronicler of white working-class woes, recently wrote: "Most of all, Trump voters want respect... [but] when they turn on the TV, they see their way of life being mocked and made fun of as nothing but uneducated white trash."

One of the most jarring revelations of the 2016 presidential election was that identity politics—normally associated with the American left—had jumped boundaries and been claimed by the white working and middle class as an ethno-nationalist movement. "Make America Great Again," meant many things to many people, but it undoubtedly included the reassertion of a particular racial and cultural identity within politics.

This surprising turn of events has led some critics to turn on identity politics itself. One is Mark Lilla, a professor of intellectual history at Columbia University, who recently claimed in The New York Times that "the age of identity liberalism must be brought to an end" because it has "produced a generation of liberals and progressives narcissistically unaware of conditions outside their self-defined groups." Needless to say, Mr. Lilla advocates abandoning identity politics as a failed project.

But this is a grave mistake. The rise of right-wing identity politics means Americans need to redouble their efforts to understand selfhood and diversity in the modern age. Perhaps no living philosopher has done more to shed light on these questions than the Catholic Canadian Charles Taylor. Mr. Taylor's reputation within contemporary philosophy is formidable. One of the most important contributors to the debates over multiculturalism in the 1990s, he became perhaps the leading thinker in the 2000s on what it means to live in a secular age.

In shortest form, what Americans can learn from Mr. Taylor is the following: The key feature of modern times is pluralism. This means the longstanding view that a secular age is one of increasing unbelief and homogenization of culture around a single set of values is wrong. Instead of homogenization, secularity means an explosion of spiritual and religious options—some traditional, others completely new.

The fact that modernity is primarily characterized by exploding diversity puts the problem of identity squarely at the center of societies like the United States. This means that when Mr. Lilla demands that identity politics "must be brought to an end" he is asking for something that runs against the basic sociological conditions of modernity. Modern people are hyperaware of the diversity of identities and this makes us fragile and insecure. Each of us knows that there are other individuals of intelligence and goodwill who pursue radically different spiritual, political and cultural conceptions of what is good.

This is in sharp contrast to premodern times. For example, in the medieval age, a peasant from Avignon was completely immersed in the horizon of his traditional world. It would have been difficult if not impossible for him to imagine his identity being radically called into jeopardy. It might even have appeared to him to be secured from time immemorial. But we moderns suffer from a very specific anxiety: We sense the radical contingency of our identities as cultural, religious, ethical and spiritual options. We sense that our identities are fragile and expressed not from time immemorial but within a bounded period of historical time. For this reason, we recognize that our identities can either succeed or fail to achieve political legitimacy and social acceptance. There is even the possibility that our identities will be eradicated.

This is what drives humans toward a very modern and heated political project: recognition. Indeed, the drive for identity recognition is perhaps the most distinctly modern political movement. As Mr. Taylor put it in one of the most important essays written on multiculturalism: "[P]eople can suffer real damage…if the people or society around them mirror back to them a confining or demeaning or contemptible picture of themselves.… Recognition is not just a courtesy we owe people. It is a vital human need."

What Mr. Lilla and Trumpists both equally fail to realize is that identity politics is not simply a self-indulgent preoccupation on the part of liberal elites. Rather, the politics of identity recognition are deeply ingrained into the modern age. Its earliest forms are

MULTICULTURALISM

Multiculturalism in the United States has a long silent history. The United States has, from its founding, taken in immigrants from different cultural backgrounds, many of whom were, at the time, controversial. First, it was the Germans who raised questions about whether they could or would become "real Americans." Then questions were raised about the Chinese and after them Irish and the Eastern European immigrants. Now it is Hispanic-Americans and Muslim-Americans of whom we ask those questions.

In every past instance those questions and, in a few limited cases, overt exclusionary policies have been overcome and those groups have become as American as descendants of Mayflower passengers. With a thoroughly thought-through effort in response to new globalized circumstances there is no reason why new ethnic and religious immigrant groups, and those that follow, cannot be as successfully integrated into American life as those that preceded them.

Which brings us to the current political version of American multiculturalism. It is a term that gathered force in the aftermath of the 1960s when cultural narcissism and identity politics became fused into the multicultural movement.

There followed group after group demanding public validation, social acceptance, and government policies to redress the historical wrongs—some very real, others exaggerated—that they used to press their claims.

It was within this contextual legacy that the multicultural demand for "recognition" gathered traction. Multiculturalism in the United States has always reflected two strands of thought. The first, more prosaic and culturally benign strand, simply stated the obvious: America is a country in which many diverse cultures exist, co-exist and find common ground as Americans.

The second more divisive strand has argued that people do, and ought to, gain their primary identities from attachment to their racial or ethnic groups. In this view the role of the government is not only to accept that "fact," but to facilitate it. Advocates of such views insist not only on their right to recognition, but also on their exclusivity along with government policies that ensure it.

"Multiculturalism In the U.S.: Cultural Narcissism and the Politics of Recognition," by Stanley Renshon, Center for Immigration Studies, February 8, 2011.

religious or nationalistic. There are movements to try to restore Christian denominations or confessional identities. There are also mobilizations to achieve the political sovereignty of a particular ethnic or cultural group—Irish, Polish, Puerto Rican, French, Lithuanians and so on. But as modernity has continued to fragment and pluralize, other groups have burst onto the scene and sought recognition as well: second-wave feminists, postcolonialists, the L.G.B.T. coalition, new age philosophies, atheists and many others. Indeed, so universal is the politics of identity that even white ethno-nationalist sites like Breitbart now (falsely) claim: "At the moment, we have identity politics for everyone except white men." (This claim is false because "white" men have had identity politics since the dawn of the modern age through particular cultural and nationalist identities.)

The politics of recognition—although it is an almost inescapable feature of modern pluralism—also has a dark side according to Taylor. Insecurity can drive a group to attempt to eliminate diversity as a way out of its sense of fragility amid pluralism. Can the force and authority of the state be used to restore the stability and dominance of a traditional identity? This seems to be the hope to which Breitbart and the more aggressive features of Trumpism appeal. Or, alternatively, perhaps the power of the state can be used as a sanction against traditional moral views in support of newer identity claims. Here parts of the liberal left have arguably overstepped their bounds.

Identity politics is in this way at the very center of the age of Trump. A whole host of writers have been warning us that the culture, faith and habits of white working-class Americans have been demeaned by the urban, liberal elite. J. D. Vance has written a much-discussed memoir, Hillbilly Elegy, about the way this scorn is felt by working-class rural families. "We're more socially isolated than ever," Mr. Vance reports, "and we pass that isolation down to our children." Likewise, many of the Christian conservatives who voted for Donald J. Trump have expressed a deep anxiety about a loss of religious liberty at the hands of those who no longer respect their views.

The backlash against this perceived sneering at white working-class and traditional identities has been undeniably severe. As part of this backlash, other identities have come under attack: Muslims, Hispanics, women, blacks, etc. These groups are increasingly targets of exclusionary rhetoric and reactionary hatred as disaffected white Americans attempt to restore a sense of lost greatness. Hate crimes are up. There is talk among some of Mr. Trump's high-profile supporters of authoritarian measures like keeping a database of "dangerous" religious minorities. The attempt to secure one's sense of identity is linked to some of the most extreme forms of mass violence in the modern world.

So, if identity politics across the political spectrum are an inescapable feature of the fragility introduced by modern pluralism, how does Charles Taylor believe modern people should respond? Should, as Mark Lilla suggests, modern people try to lessen the significance of their identities when it comes to politics? Mr. Taylor suggests a different approach. Basically, debates in society need to be about what constitutes a reasonable amount of pluralism. From this perspective, the big trap American politics has fallen into in recent decades is attempting to canonize particular ethical or moral views through the state (for example, the heated battle over traditional versus gay marriage, or the similar one going on over bathrooms). American politics has been playing a dangerous game, where identities on all sides feel existentially menaced by each new election. Under this analysis, Trumpism is simply the most extreme expression of this anxiety to date.

Instead of terrorizing each other with control of the state every four years, Americans might spend more time finding ways to accommodate a diversity of identities across the political spectrum. The federal government would have a role to play in securing certain rights, but local governments would also allow for different communities to live out their diverse ethics. Rather than trying to create a national moral monoculture through the courts (which misunderstands the meaning of our secular age) Mr. Taylor's brand of multiculturalism seeks to protect a diversity of religious and spiritual options.

All this implies a rather surprising way of looking at how democracies work well in the modern age. Contrary to the view that agreement around human rights is achieved by homogenizing toward a single dominant ethic ("Judeo-Christianity" for conservatives, or "secular progressivism" for liberals, or some version of Enlightenment liberalism for Mr. Lilla), consensus is achieved by allowing for creative re-immersion in particular traditions. We urgently need to reassess what we understand by being "modern" people. Among other things, across the political spectrum we need to become far more comfortable with the cultural and philosophical role of traditions and pluralism. To be an advocate of modern, secular societies, then, means to embrace a pluralism that includes both the traditional identities of the white working class and Muslims, of evangelicals and the L.G.B.T. coalition.

In a recent feature in The New Yorker, Mr. Taylor was quoted as saying that dialogue with opponents in the age of Trump is deeply in need of three simple, humble steps: First, "try to listen"; second, "find out what's troubling" your opponent; and third, "stop condemning." In this, Mr. Taylor's Catholic-informed ethic is very close to that of the current pope, who has repeatedly advised Christians that they need to develop "in a special way, the capacity to dialogue and encounter." In other words, contra Mr. Lilla, American society is going to have to become much more comfortable with the deep diversity of identity politics across the entire spectrum of society if it is to fare any better in the coming year than it did in 2016.

> "*The identity politics industry that has provided so many perks and privileges in academia and elsewhere will find itself under siege from the left, from a genuine movement of the working class and the resurgence of the class struggle.*"

Class Should Be an Integral Part of Identity Politics

Fred Mazelis

In the following viewpoint, Fred Mazelis argues that class is too often neglected in political discussions. He criticizes the columnist and political writer Michael Eric Dyson for focusing on race to the exclusion of class. In the wake of Donald Trump's presidential victory, Mazelis argues that race in itself was not the deciding factor, just as the "white working class" should not be blamed for Trump's election. Rather, this focus on race excludes the integral conversation on class and, particularly, the exclusion of poor and working-class groups from the US political arena in favor of a small group of elites. Mazelis is a founding member of the Worker's League and has been a third-party vice presidential candidate for the Socialist Equality Party.

As you read, consider the following questions:

1. What is Mazelis's criticism of columnist Michael Eric Dyson?
2. What is the author's complaint about Dyson's portrayal of himself as a representative of "Black America"?
3. What was Dyson's criticism of "working class solidarity," according to the viewpoint?

Michael Eric Dyson's latest column, on the front page of the Sunday, December 18 editorial section of the *New York Times*, extends the venomous attacks of the practitioners of identity politics on those who dare to question the view that race is the fundamental dividing line in American society.

Dyson, a Georgetown University professor, author and regular contributor to the *Times*, headlines his article, "Donald Trump's Racial Ignorance." Within a few paragraphs, however, it becomes clear that his real target is not Donald Trump at all, but rather the working class.

Pundits and Democratic politicians alike have struggled to come up with explanations for the evaporation of the Clinton electoral victory they had so confidently predicted. The dominant line, championed by the *Times* and also by both Bill and Hillary Clinton in recent weeks, is that "Russian hacking" and the last-minute intervention of FBI Director James Comey on the issue of Clinton's emails combined to deliver key battleground states to the Republican nominee.

Many millions of people are not buying this unlikely explanation, however. In the weeks since the election, it has become increasingly clear that Trump's success was due largely to his ability to pose as the "anti-establishment candidate," a pose made possible only by both the reactionary record of the Obama administration and the right-wing campaign of Hillary Clinton.

Major sections of the corporate media and the ruling elite, committed to the identity politics strategy that was, along with war-mongering against Russia, the sum total of Clinton's campaign, have mounted a defense of their racialist and gender-based appeals, even as they continue their hysteria on Russian hacking and its supposedly enormous impact.

Dyson is part of the identity politics counterattack. There is only one subject he wishes to discuss, and that is race. He accuses Trump of "not knowing" black people, but then he continues, "Mr. Trump is not alone in this deliberate ignorance, as postelection calls on the left to forget about identity politics have shown…The road ahead is not easy, primarily because Mr. Trump's ignorance about race, his critical lack of nuance and learning about it, exists among liberals and the white left, too."

Dyson zeroes in on 2016 presidential aspirant Bernie Sanders, who won more than 13 million votes in the primaries, only slightly fewer than Clinton, by declaring himself a "democratic socialist" and calling for a "political revolution" against the billionaires.

"From the start of his 2016 presidential campaign," Dyson writes, "Bernie Sanders was prickly about race, uncomfortable with an outspoken, demanding blackness, resistant to letting go of his preference for discussing class over race. … Mr. Sanders seemed to remain at heart a man of the people, especially if those people were the white working class."

One should note the sarcasm with which Dyson drops the phrase "man of the people." He portrays himself as a representative of "black America," but Dyson is, in fact, a political representative of only one thin section of the African-American population, the upper-middle class. The *Times* columnist owes his allegiance to the ruling elite and has nothing but contempt for the working class of all races and ethnicities.

Dyson is outraged at Sanders's timid recent suggestion that it may be necessary to "go beyond identity politics." He quotes Sanders as saying that it is "very easy for many Americans to say, I hate racism, I hate homophobia, I hate sexism," but "a little bit harder for people in the middle or upper-middle class to say, maybe we do have to deal with the greed of Wall Street."

This, according to Dyson, is "a nifty bit of historical revisionism," since, he claims, "for the longest time there was little consideration of diversity…among liberal elites."

It is Dyson who is guilty of revisionism, if not worse. For more than 40 years, the US ruling class has embraced the mantra of diversity and programs such as affirmative action. Far from liberal elites avoiding this approach, it has been a key element of the social counterrevolution over the past four decades: attacking the jobs and living standards of the working class while elevating a privileged layer of blacks, Latinos, women and gays into the ranks of corporate management, political office, academia, the labor bureaucracy and the media.

The ruling class and both capitalist parties, beginning with Nixon's "black capitalism" almost five decades ago, have fomented divisions on the basis of race. Nixon combined his cynical use of "affirmative action" with the notorious "Southern strategy," aimed at shifting the remnants of the Jim Crow establishment to the Republican Party. This was followed by various other techniques, including the law-and-order campaigns of the 1980s and 1990s.

Meanwhile, the Democrats, reflecting the impossibility of any program of even modest social reform under decaying American capitalism, abandoned even the hint of an appeal to workers based on the defense and extension of the social programs of the 1930s and 1960s. The two parties worked out an unspoken and filthy division of labor, in which the Democrats were allowed to posture as defenders of the black, Hispanic and immigrant population, while white workers were increasingly labeled as "privileged" and ceded to the Republicans.

Bernie Sanders is, of course, no representative of the working class. His differences with both Clinton and Dyson are only tactical. Sanders meekly accepted the nomination of Clinton and obediently lined up in support of her campaign. And he is continuing his efforts, after the election fiasco for the Democrats, to channel mass opposition to Trump and Wall Street back into this party of big business and war.

It is not primarily Sanders that worries Dyson. He cannot forget the millions who voted for Sanders precisely because of the fact that, in Dyson's words, he was guilty of "discussing class over race." All these voters—masses of workers and young people—not to mention the even greater number who didn't vote because they were thoroughly disgusted with both big-business parties, were not "turned off" by the talk of "class." Dyson's attack on Sanders for daring to speak of "the greed of Wall Street" makes very clear his own alignment—with Wall Street.

Dyson closes with an attack on "working class solidarity," which he calls "a cover…to combat racial, sexual and gender progress." Here he makes explicit his hostility to the working class and his use of racial politics to attack and divide the working class on behalf of the ruling elite.

Dyson and the whole layer for which he speaks fear that the decades in which identity politics has been largely unchallenged except by the Marxist movement are coming to an end. The identity politics industry that has provided so many perks and privileges in academia and elsewhere will find itself under siege from the left, from a genuine movement of the working class and the resurgence of the class struggle.

Those disgusted by the identity politics campaign of Hillary Clinton were by no means confined to white workers, some of whom voted for Trump in protest or disgust. Millions of black, Hispanic and immigrant workers stayed home (and some even voted for Trump), because they were also disgusted with eight years of growing inequality and continuous war under Obama, and Clinton's promise to continue his policies.

It is the stirrings in the working class that have Dyson and the editors and publishers of the *Times*, along with the rest of the media, increasingly worried. They are working overtime to change the subject from class to race, from the collapse of the vote for the Wall Street Democrats to the supposed "whitelash" that elected Trump.

> *"Those who see themselves as perennial victims also feel very comfortable, when they express their feelings of being oppressed, in projecting that same victimization outward on their oppressors."*

Identity Politics Has Eroded Free Speech

Richard L. Cravatts

In the following viewpoint, Richard L. Cravatts argues that identity politics has resulted in a decline in free speech, particularly in academic settings. He attributes this to the compartmentalization of identities that identity politics has contributed to, which has led to people refusing to listen to others who might have a different worldview than they do. To support his claim, Cravatts cites the reaction that occurred at the University of California, Berkeley in 2017 when Milo Yiannopoulos, a political commentator associated with the alt-right movement, was invited to speak on campus. Eventually, because of university-wide protests, Yiannopoulos's event was canceled. Cravatts is immediate past-president of scholars for Peace in the Middle East (SPME) and the author of Dispatches From the Campus War Against Israel and Jews.*

"Berkeley, Identity Politics, and the Progressive Assault On Campus Free Speech," by Richard L. Cravatts, Scholars for Peace in the Middle East, February 7, 2017. Reprinted by permission.

As you read, consider the following questions:

1. What was the theme of Yiannopoulos's speech supposed to be?
2. Do you agree that "victimism" may lead to a smaller worldview?
3. Do you think the language Cravatt uses—such as calling liberals "brats"—works for or against his argument?

O f the many intellectual perversions currently taking root on college campuses, perhaps none is more contradictory to what should be one of higher education's core values than the suppression of free speech. With alarming regularity, speakers are shouted down, booed, jeered, and barraged with vitriol, all at the hands of progressive groups who give lip service to the notion of academic free speech, and who demand it when their own speech is at issue, but have no interest in listening to, or letting others listen to, ideas that contradict their own world view.

This is the tragic and inevitable result of decades of grievance-based victimism by self-designated groups who frame their rights and demands on identity politics. Those who see themselves as perennial victims also feel very comfortable, when they express their feelings of being oppressed, in projecting that same victimization outward on their oppressors, as witnessed recently, for example, at Berkeley University where some 1500 violent rioters, including members of the radical, far-Left Antifa group, feminists, gay activists, pro-immigration groups, and other faculty and students, lit fires, smashed windows, tossed smoke bombs, destroyed property, and pepper sprayed and beat pro-Trump bystanders and conservatives, all because of the purported extreme ideology of Milo Yiannopoulos, a speaker invited to campus by the Berkeley College Republicans that evening as part of his "The Dangerous Faggot Tour."

Lost in the reporting about the Berkeley rioting, of course, is the topic that was to be the theme of Yiannopoulos' February 1st speech. It was specifically to address Berkeley's recent decision, along with approximately 30 other campuses across the country, to become "sanctuary campuses," giving them the dubious distinction of flaunting the intent and spirit of federal law that could lead to the arrest of students who are attending schools in this country but are actually not legally permitted to do so. Yiannopoulos was also going to raise the related, and clearly relevant, question of whether, once they had, in contravention of current law, declared themselves either sanctuary cities of sanctuary campuses, these entities should lose Federal funding.

Interestingly, in sending a letter to the university community prior to the Yiannopoulos' planned speech, Berkeley's Chancellor, Nicholas Dirks, confirmed, on one hand, a "right to free expression, enshrined in the First Amendment to the U.S. Constitution and reflected in some of the most important moments of Berkeley's history," but then portrayed Yiannopoulos in that letter as "a troll and provocateur who uses odious behavior in part to 'entertain,' but also to deflect any serious engagement with ideas," clearly signaling to readers that, as far as the Berkeley administration was concerned, this speech would be in violation of the prevailing norms and beliefs of the University at large and would, consequently, have no intrinsic intellectual value.

So while Dirks was purportedly supporting the idea of academic free speech, together with its oft-lauded vigorous open debate, he actually was violating the content neutrality that is required of free speech on campuses by leaving no one reading his letter with any doubt as to where he and the University stood on this issue, especially since the decision had already been made to ignore existing statutes that would call for the arrest and possible deportation of individuals who attend schools in this country but are not legally permitted to do so.

The debate over whether immigration to this country should continue without proper vetting and oversight, of course, was one of the central issues of the recent presidential election, so there is considerable emotion and debate over this topic, especially among college students and faculty (not to mention Democrat governors and mayors across the country), who have taken it upon themselves to decide that they have greater moral authority to settle this issue than the government does in enforcing existing laws of this nation.

Sixty million people, nearly half of the total population who voted in the presidential election, decided that this issue was certainly worthy of debate, and the notion that Berkeley, its leadership, and some of its faculty and students had unilaterally decided that sanctuary campuses were not only a good idea but something that they could implement—in violation of law—is certainly a topic that was worthy of being challenged by a speaker like Yiannopoulos.

The Berkeley event exposes one of the dangers of suppressing certain types of speech on campus, where progressive social justice warriors feel morally empowered to decide who can say what about whom, and have taken it upon themselves to exclude and suppress certain types of speech and certain topics which they have collectively decided cannot and should not be discussed.

No one is interested in suppressing the corrosive and unhelpful speech of these ideological brats, who preen self-righteously about their unabridged right to champion progressive aims and anti-Trump, pro-Left ideology. Similar to the anti-Israel activists who have hijacked academic debate about the Middle East, Leftist students and faculty—at Berkeley and elsewhere– have been very free and successful in exploiting the protection of academic free speech to advance their toxic views on campuses, yet simultaneously decry that same freedom when used by those with opposing—very often stronger and more truthful—views.

These sanctimonious activists may well feel that they have access to all the truth and facts, but even if this were true—which it demonstrably and regularly is not—it does not empower them with the right to have the only voice to trumpet their ideology and to disrupt, shout down, or totally eliminate competing opinions in political or academic debates. No one individual or group has the moral authority or intellectual might to decide what may and may not be discussed, and especially young, sanctimonious students—whose expertise and knowledge about immigration, national security, and terrorism is frequently characterized by distortions, lies, lack of context, corrosive bias against democracies, and errors in history, law, and facts.

College administrators regularly give lip service to the enshrined value of academic free speech and robust debate about controversial issues, and that is an admirable goal and an intellectual environment in which scholarship and learning can thrive. But university communities also thrive when they operate with civility and decorum, meaning that when it comes to academic free speech, students and faculty have the right to express their ideas, no matter how controversial, but, importantly, they must also ensure that this speech takes place in what the courts in First Amendment cases have referred to as an appropriate "time, place, and manner."

This means that it was never the intended purpose of academic free speech to enable or permit students, for example, to scream out in protest in classrooms if they disagree with the instructor or merely wish to raise their displeasure with some issue, engage in speech and behavior that would normally be considered to be incitement or harassment or criminal, and, most relevant to this current issue, individuals cannot, under the protection of free speech, deprive another of his or her free speech rights—through disruptions, heckling, physical obstructions, or other tactics which have as their purpose to suppress and/or eliminate the speech of those with opposing views.

Most universities, of course, have codes of conduct which proscribe inappropriate speech and behavior, as does Berkeley, whose own Code of Student Conduct would punish the protesters who disrupted Yiannopoulos' speech because "Some forms of speech are not constitutionally protected and may be grounds for discipline," including "threats of violence, incitement to imminent lawless action, raising false alarms regarding imminent personal danger, and certain severe and pervasive harassment." It was never the purpose of academic free speech, from either a legal or moral standpoint, to allow whiny intellectual thugs to determine which ideas could be aired and which could not—a fascistic tactic that has no place in the academy where at least the pretense of scholarly inquiry and debate still remains.

And the other, oft-expressed accusation that counter-speech to this activism is merely a disingenuous effort on the part of conservatives to suppress and "chill" the free speech of these arrogant, sententious anti-Trump progressives is yet another attempt to neutralize and eliminate an opposing view, deeming it malicious in its intent and therefore undeserving of attention. Because they most likely know that their arguments and ideology are defective and cannot stand up to the scrutiny that an actual vigorous debate will bring, these self-professed champions of free speech, in reality, wish for that privilege and right to be enjoyed only by them.

"The peculiar evil of silencing the expression of an opinion is," observed John Stuart Mill in On Liberty, "that . . . [i]f the opinion is right, [individuals] are deprived of the opportunity of exchanging error for truth: if wrong, they lose, what is almost as great a benefit, the clearer perception and livelier impression of truth, produced by its collision with error."

True intellectual diversity—the ideal that is often bandied about but rarely achieved—must be dedicated to the protection of unfettered speech, representing opposing viewpoints, where the best ideas become clear through the utterance of weaker ones. Universities, if they truly believe that academic free speech helps achieve "the clearer perception and livelier impression of truth," must ensure that rights to expression are not trampled on by those whose ideology is so virulent that they are unable, and unwilling, to, as Mill put it, "exchange error for truth."

> *"Identity politics, and ideas derived from it such as privilege theory and intersectionality, have produced possibly the lowest level and most simplistic understanding of class consciousness in the history of modern capitalism."*

We Need a Marxist Identity Politics

Albert L. Terry, III

In the following viewpoint, Albert L. Terry argues that identity politics will soon become obsolete, particularly as people realize that individual identities are not as useful without an overarching framework of social class and class struggle. For Terry, it is important to develop an intersectional and particularly Marxist view of political movements. He states, "What we should bring to light, however, is that it's not just about the intersection between racial, gender, and sexual identity, but between all those AND class identity." Terry contends that while one identity should not trump another, all identities are constrained by capitalist forms of government and elitism and thus can be reunited under the banner of class struggle. Terry is founding member of Mobile Bay Socialist Collective and co-chair of treasury of the Alabama Green Party.

"A Few Words On Marxism and Identity Politics," by Albert L. Terry, III, Left Voice, January 8, 2017. Reprinted by permission.

As you read, consider the following questions:

1. What recent examples does the author use to support his argument that identity politics has failed?
2. Why does the author state that identity politics will become irrelevant?
3. How does the author relate identity to class struggle? Do you agree or disagree with his analysis?

The year 2016 will be remembered as the year that identity politics, as it is commonly understood, began the long descent into irrelevancy.

The fact that the past eight years under the first black president saw conditions grow objectively worse for Black America has challenged the idea that a politician—simply by merit of being black—innately has the best interests of black people at heart. Then, of course, there was Hillary Clinton's presidential campaign, in which efforts to literally rewrite history and frame Clinton as a feminist champion of women's rights fell completely flat; fifty-four percent of women voters went with Clinton, almost the same percentage that voted Obama in 2012. Despite running against a raging misogynist that has been accused of multiple sexual assaults, as well as the rape of his then-wife Ivana in 1989, Hillary did no better than Obama amongst women. Needless to say, not many people bought the idea that Hillary would look out for women simply because she is a woman.

Now that this critical juncture has been reached, the socialist left can rejoice. Identity politics, and ideas derived from it such as privilege theory and intersectionality, have produced possibly the lowest level and most simplistic understanding of class consciousness in the history of modern capitalism. Right now we are presented with our best opportunity in decades to counteract the influence of these ideas and bring Marxist class analysis back to the fore. The only problem with that is the part where we counteract identity.

Leftists who put forth an analysis in which politics is entirely about class and not in any way about race, gender, or sexuality tend not to capture many hearts and minds, and there is one important reason for that: their analysis is wrong.

Now hear me out, Marxists absolutely should be criticizing the school of identity politics that has reigned heretofore. Let's call this liberal or corporate identity politics—because this school, despite its radical beginnings amongst late-Civil-Rights-era and Black Power organizations, has by now been thoroughly co-opted by "progressive Democrat"-run NGO think tanks. Liberal identity politics deserves criticism for omitting class analysis from its evaluation of how oppression works, for pursuing individualist goals to become part of the bourgeois class rather than dismantle it, for being so blind to history and to the nature of capitalism as to think that this amounts to "liberation," for subsuming movements under any Democratic Party politician willing to pay lip service to one minority group or another, and for not moving a muscle when said politician sacrifices said group's interests on the altar of "bipartisanship" or "compromise." The problem is that there seem to be very few criticisms that include an analysis like the one above (with notable exceptions like Adolph Reed's essays on the subject), and mostly ones that sound like angry (usually) white people projecting their irritation at the assertion that they hold societal privilege, or at having been told themselves to "check their privilege" by some snotty kid new to left activism.

Again, we have every right to be angry at the mistaken idea that oppression is completely about race/gender/sexuality, not class. However, to simply flip that equation on its head and assert that it's all about class, and not about race, gender, or sexuality is an egregious mistake, especially from anyone claiming to provide a materialist analysis. To counter interpretations of privilege theory by arguing that there is no white, male, cis-, or hetero- privilege is to ignore the material realities of capitalist society.

That argument ignores the fact that black and brown people still face indiscriminate violence and higher rates of unreasonable search and seizure at the hands of police (on the day I began typing this, the Charlotte-Mecklenburg PD ruled that an officer was justified in murdering Keith Lamont Scott) than even the poorest whites. That black and brown people languish under a system of mass incarceration, literally enslaving them and forcing them to labor for corporations and state governments for pennies an hour (if any pay at all). That the dire economic conditions becoming increasingly prevalent in working class white communities are and have been a fact of life in working class POC communities even during times of relative economic prosperity.

It also ignores the fact that women, on average, are paid 77 cents for every dollar a man makes, and that they still perform an overwhelming majority of unpaid domestic labor. That far too many people still view women as property and that the consequent slut-shaming, rape culture, and victim-blaming result in an alarming percentage of women being sexually assaulted at least once in their lifetimes.

It ignores the fact that LGBTQIA people are still subject to being fired from their jobs in right-to-work states just for being LGBTQIA as long as their employer is smart enough not to explicitly state that a person is being fired for their gender or sexual identity. That twenty-six transgender people were murdered in 2016 just for being who they are and that LGBTQIA people are statistically the most likely targets of hate crimes (see Pulse massacre of June 2016).

To rephrase all that more concisely, it's "All Lives Matter," but for alleged Marxists who are severely out-of-touch and out-of-date.

Capitalism has survived this long only by erecting barriers between working people; stratifying us into little boxes to more easily oppress us each individually, placing special forms of oppression on certain groups, and propagandizing us into believing that the problem is the people next to us and not the ones lording over us. The thing about that though: Capitalism is a white supremacist, misogynistic, cisnormative, heteronormative system, meaning that those special layers of oppression are reserved for those who are not white, not men, not cisgendered, and not heterosexual.

This is why these little tantrums railing against privilege theory are wrong. Even if you do face the oppression that comes with poverty, if you are white or male or cisgendered or straight, you do benefit from a relative sort of privilege (bonus points for two or more). Not because people that are poor but meet at least one of these criteria are no longer oppressed, but because they have the privilege of being unlikely to have their brains blown out [or bashed in] by police [or fascists] for selling cigarettes or walking in the street or reaching for their wallet or, you know, just having the audacity to exist.

Given these very basic facts, we need to shape our understanding of Marxism to take into account what role identity plays in the consciousness of working people. We also need to recognize the role that the identity-specific forms of oppression faced by POC, LGBTQIA people, and women play in upholding capitalism in the U.S. (aptly called the "breadbasket of capitalism") today, because the two are related. Insisting that we need to just drop these barriers of identity and all identify only as working class, or else the revolution will fail, makes you sound like one of those "colorblind" folks we leftists love to hate (and for good reason).

I am a black man of working class background, I am also a Marxist. Frankly, if you tell me that struggles against racism need to take a backseat to whatever overgeneralized idea of working class struggle you're advocating, I'm going to tell you to eat a bullet. Stop using Marxism as a cover for your personal discomfort at having to talk about race, gender, or sexuality. Marxism is scientific, so suggesting that specific struggles based on race/gender/sexual identity are of lesser importance in a society built on the subjugation of race/gender/sexual minorities isn't just bad politics, it's outright contrary to the idea of Marxism.

We have to realize that the struggles we are facing are, in fact, intersectional (I know you hate that word, probably about as much as I hate whitewashed Marxism). What we should bring to light, however, is that it's not just about the intersection between racial, gender, and sexual identity, but between all those AND class identity. We need to put forward a new, Marxist identity politics that recognizes the special oppression that comes with race and the consequent importance of fighting racism head-on, but also emphasizes that the interests of the bourgeoisie and petit bourgeoisie of color are just as hostile to working class POC as the interests of the white bourgeoisie are and that the interests of bourgeois women are still hostile to the interests of working class women. Class and identity are not mutually exclusive: black and brown workers' struggle is workers' struggle; working women's struggle is workers' struggle; LGBTQIA workers' struggle is workers' struggle. The sooner some of y'all come to realize that, the sooner we can rise up together and overthrow this capitalism bullshit for good. Now, let's do better.

Periodical and Internet Sources Bibliography

The following articles have been selected to supplement the diverse views presented in this chapter.

Marcie Bianco, "What Hillary Clinton Gets That Bernie Sanders Doesn't: Identity Politics," *Quartz*, April 19, 2016, https://qz.com/664475/hillary-clinton-understands-that-a-political-revolution-is-not-one-size-fits-all.

David Eaton, "Resentment, Multiculturalism, and Identity Politics," *Applied Unificiationism*, February 27, 2017, https://appliedunificationism.com/2017/02/27/resentment-multiculturalism-and-identity-politics.

Jonathan Dean, "Who's Afraid of Identity Politics," London School of Economics and Political Science Blogs, December 9, 2016, http://blogs.lse.ac.uk/politicsandpolicy/whos-afraid-of-identity-politics.

Jonah Goldberg, "The Folly of White Identity Politics," *National Review*, August 18, 2016, http://www.nationalreview.com/corner/439150/white-identity-politics-wrong-and-immoral.

Peter Lewis, "Looking Through a Marxist Lens (and Why Class is the New Black)," *Guardian*, November 29, 2016, https://www.theguardian.com/commentisfree/2016/nov/30/looking-through-a-marxist-lens-and-why-class-is-the-new-black.

Ben Norton, "Adolph Reed: Identity Politics Is Neoliberalism," BenNorton.com, June 29, 2015, https://bennorton.com/adolph-reed-identity-politics-is-neoliberalism.

James Petras, "A Marxist Critique of Post-Marxism," *Rebelion*, November 1997, https://www.rebelion.org/hemeroteca/petras/english/critique170102.htm.

Michael Rectenwald, "What's Wrong with Identity Politics (and Intersectionality Theory)? A Response to Mark Fisher's "Exiting the Vampire Castle" (And Its Critics), *North Star*, December 2, 2013, http://www.thenorthstar.info/?p=11411.

Kelton Sears and Asad Haider, "A Marxist Critiques Identity Politics," *Portside*, April 25, 2017, http://portside.org/2017-04-26/marxist-critiques-identity-politics.

OPPOSING
VIEWPOINTS®
SERIES

CHAPTER 4

How Can Identity Politics Become a More Useful Political Organizing Tool in the Future?

Chapter Preface

The authors in this chapter look to the future, both in optimism and despair, to find a place for identity politics in the American political system. For some commentators, like Ben Debney, identity politics should largely be eschewed for effective progressive political organizing to take place. According to Debney, identity politics shares much in common with white supremacy and this hypocrisy at the basis of liberal platforms is leading to lost elections.

Similarly, Douglas Williams criticizes identity politics for its exclusive, rather than inclusive, nature. But, rather than throwing out the baby with the bathwater, Williams suggests that identity politics can be reformed to become more inclusive.

Ron Daniels and M. J. Kaplan take more optimistic positions in regard to identity politics, with Daniels stating that identity politics has largely been useful and is feared and criticized because of its political power and Kaplan seeing a new form of identity politics manifest in the Women's March on Washington in 2017.

Finally, two commentators look forward to the end of identity politics as we know it. Victor Davis Hanson argues that identity politics is in its death throes due to our new genetic reality. As the world has become more interconnected, different races and ethnicities have mixed. Soon, Hanson states, "pure" whites, in the terms of the alt-right, will no longer exist and ethnic and racial intermixing will make it hard to distinguish groups of people.

Michael Lind takes a different approach in the last viewpoint of the chapter, stating that a political revolution is at hand that will change the focus of identity politics from who we are to where we live. For Lind, social conservativism is dying as the millennial generation comes to power. This means that ethnic, racial, gender, and sexual identities will bear less weight than a belief in the role of government dictated largely by where one lives.

> *"In fact, a truly bizarre and arguably telling feature of identity politics as it appears on the left are the shared commonalities in terms of basic assumptions and subjective dynamics with identity politics as a feature of white supremacism."*

Leftist Identity Politics Shares Much in Common with White Supremacy

Ben Debney

In the following viewpoint, Ben Debney analyzes the victory of Donald Trump in the 2016 US presidential election and the failings of the Democratic Party. He states that the Democratic Party wrongly assumed that women would vote for Hillary Clinton, thus "banking" on the importance of identity politics. However, Debney states that it is this focus on identity politics that not only has led to Democratic losses, but also has shown the left's inability to see how their brand of identity politics is not unlike white supremacists' brand of identity politics. For Debney, identity politics must be done away with for liberals to come out ahead in elections—and to distance themselves from the dangerous views they see on the ultra-right. Debney is a PhD candidate in international relations at Deakin University, in Australia. He is studying moral panics and the political economy of scapegoating.

"The Paradox of Identity Politics," by Ben Debney, CounterPunch, March 16, 2017. Reprinted by permission.

As you read, consider the following questions:

1. Why does the author state that Democrats "banked" on Hillary Clinton to win the 2016 US presidential election because of identity politics?

2. Why is white supremacism one of the least demanding of ideologies, according to the viewpoint?

3. What does the author mean by the left's identity politics "'Oppression Olympics' routine"?

A recent piece on *Voices of the Revolution*, "The Siren Song of Identity Politics," properly attempts a critique of liberal identity politics, but rather than effectively addressing the issue, veers disastrously towards the basic operating assumptions of white supremacists. This is a shame; the question is a very important one. The Democratic Party has yet, after all, to properly account for the inability of their candidate to beat a troglodyte like Donald Trump.

Given the horror show that Trump's ascendency to the Presidency has very quickly become, it would seem incumbent to prevent further repeats of same. This is truer again when we consider that his win was less a popular endorsement of his campaign than a loss for the Democrats, who banked—mistakenly as it turns out—on identity politics to get Clinton across the line.

In fact, fifty-three percent of white women voters in disagreed that Clinton's gender was her main selling point, or more surprisingly that Trump's "grab 'em by the pussy" misogyny and ringing endorsement of sexual assault wasn't enough for him to be roundly rejected. If the possibility of having the first woman president or the markedly sociopathic tendencies of the successful candidate weren't enough to decide the election, then a rethink is well nigh.

In the name of such, Frank Doyle argues that basic problem with modern liberalism lies in a paradox apparent in the dynamics between the "Black Lives Matter" movement and the "counter-cry," "All Lives Matter." This paradox, he claims, derives from the fact that 'cultural attention is a zero-sum game, and that since "the news can only push so many stories," and "the public only has so much time to think about societal problems," the necessary result is that, "For one group to get more attention, another must get less."

The upshot of this, says Doyle, is the resentment from whites that forms the basis of the "All Lives Matter" movement. "Why," he asks, "should a single demographic receive such focus when there are problems that affect everyone?" While the government "must triage these problems," the fact appears to be that "no course of action here would do justice to all those involved."

This being the case, he continues, we should focus not on who are affected by these issues, since this is "inherently divisive and a demonstrably losing proposition for the Democratic Party," but instead of turning "criminal justice reform into a 'black people problem,'" and "Midwestern job loss to automation and outsourcing into a 'white people problem,'" should rather "bring the focus back to the issues themselves."

Progressives must return the public focus to the universal validity of progressive policies and principles, not to the inherently divisive issue of who gets the most out of them. We should prioritize based on the significance of the ideal in its own right, not on the count or demographic of those it affects . . . We cannot afford to repeat the mistakes of this election. We cannot afford to alienate a massive demographic due to divisive rhetoric a second time.

This is a very odd stance to take towards the causes of Clinton's election loss. Why does Doyle choose to focus on Black Lives Matter of all things, and not for example the close and long-standing ties between the Democratic candidate and Wall St? Trump rightly criticized Clinton for her ties to Wall St and was in fact able to capitalize heavily off it—his own egregious hypocrisy on that count notwithstanding.

Why for that matter did he not mention Clinton's hawkish foreign policy record during the Obama years, which was nothing if not amenable to privileged elites—the fossil fuel and armament industries in particular? As Gary Leupp points out,

The "surge" in Afghanistan; the winding down of the Iraq occupation; the huge increase in drone strikes in Pakistan and Afghanistan, killing hundreds of civilians and terrorizing whole regions; the total failure of the Obama administration to end U.S. client state Israel's illegal settlements on the West Bank and indeed a general deterioration in high-level U.S.-Israeli relations; various U.S. interventions during the "Arab Spring;" the U.S./NATO assault on Libya that destroyed that modern state, etc.? Hillary was a key player in all these events. It's all in her record, for all to see.

One might contend that it was this record, one that made her indistinguishable from Bush-era neoconservatives—many of whom tellingly supported her candidature—that, coupled with her close ties to Wall St., accounts for her loss. Indeed, and as noted, fifty-three percent of white female votes agreed, voting for the short-fingered vulgarian.

Where Black Lives Matter fits into these issues is hard to gather; if anything, the problematizing of this movement as "divisive" echoes the kinds of sentiments we can find at places like Breitbart, which insists that "nobody is claiming that black lives DON'T matter!" (though they are, by silencing black voices with victim blaming, in the manner that Breitbart writers for one like to carry on with as a matter of course) and that, contrary to "garish example of Identity Politics run amok," there "simply isn't a pro-death, pro-murdering, or pro-killing black people movement anywhere on the political landscape" (though there is, and they're called the police). Factual objections are for the moment beside the point; what is the point are the features common to both arguments.

In the case of racisms perpetrated by websites like Breitbart, for example, the problematizing of Black Lives Matter serves to blame minorities for wanting to be visible; trying to approach police violence as "an issue that affects everybody" in the name of not succumbing to the shortcomings of identity politics is to neglect the fact (1) that extra-judicial killings occur disproportionately against nonwhites, and (2) the color line upon which class hierarchies have been constructed historically—a fact that tends to be true incidentally anywhere around the world where Europeans have set foot. To look to whitewash history in the name of electoral success is to blame Black Lives Matter for acknowledging that racial divisions exist by labelling them as "divisive" for speaking up, and thus to try to oppose racism by adopting it.

Not only is this not an effective strategy for people who identify as progressive over the longer term, it also fails to address the problem of identity politics and the part it plays in the failures of the left to form an effective counter-power to Trump's feral corporatism. Perhaps even more paradoxically, it tend to invoke the kinds of actually-existing identity politics that are a characteristic feature of white supremacism; it is the crowning heights of hypocrisy for racists and white supremacists to carry on about the perils of identity politics when it comes to acknowledging various forms of social and economic privilege, and to then base an entire ideology —indeed, their entire identity—on their status as whites.

In fact, a truly bizarre and arguably telling feature of identity politics as it appears on the left are the shared commonalities in terms of basic assumptions and subjective dynamics with identity politics as a feature of white supremacism. In white supremacism, white identity is the starting point for assumptions of relative merit —the opinions and beliefs of whites are of inherently greater value simply because of their identity. Furthermore, they don't need facts or proofs to support their ideological claims because their identity *is* their argument, one that conveniently enough requires no further evidencing or substantiation.

Thanks to these facets of white supremacist identity politics, is no more possible to demand supporting evidence from white supremacists than it is to express doubt in, contradict, question or challenge their guiding assumptions without being identified with the enemy. In this sense of course, white supremacism is probably one of the least demanding ideologies on the planet, requiring nothing more than our circumstances of birth (which those of us who are white clearly had no say in) to justify feelings of worth and merit that again as a characteristic feature require no investment in terms of time, energy or effort to earn.

Identity politics on the left operate much the same way. Actual political arguments will acknowledge the intersectional relationship between various hierarchies of privilege-based injustice and oppression, noting at the root of these a predatory and generally sociopathic gaze that sees workers, women, the flora and fauna and even the Earth itself as simple objects who exist solely to be used and abused as the predator sees fit and whose sole value resides in their exploitability for profit. Identity politics invoked in the name of such arguments suggests that, because I belong to one of the categories objectified and targeted for exploitation, that I have the right to invoke the same kinds of attitudes and relations that oppress me for the sake of stealing a few crumbs from the table of coercion.

Such attitudes are patently visible in such areas as the Leninist strategy of vanguardism, which as a matter of definition tries to resolve ideological controversies and other disagreements by asserting a particular kind of identity—in this instance, that of the working class, or of those who appoint themselves to speak in their name at least. I represent the working class, says Leninist vanguardism, therefore as a matter of definition you can't contradict me without being against the working class.

This attitude, the one based on the logic that says "if you think for yourself the enemies of the working class win," is no different from the point of view of its blame-shifting and victim-blaming mechanics than the attitude of white supremacists that, "if you think for yourself, the enemies of the white race win." While the purported evil is different—each of these positions ironically enough referring in fact to the other—they are otherwise perfectly alike. More to the point, they serve the same function, which is to compel obedience to the ideological dictates of the particular form of identity politics (and, naturally, the person invoking them). If you don't shut your mouth and do as you're told, you're evil.

Historical examples illustrate this dynamic well enough. In 1934 the head of the Leningrad Soviet, Sergei Kirov, was assassinated in Moscow by what historians tend to agree were likely agents of the GPU, the state secret police and forerunners of the KGB. Stalin immediately set on this highly convenient assassination of his closest political rival and used it as the basis for a panic driven by the state media about a "fifth column" of counter-revolutionary, reactionary Trotskyist terrorists who were trying to overthrow the glorious socialist utopia he had bequeathed to the Russian people and restore Tsarism and capitalism.

This was of course a complete myth, but one that Stalin used as the basis for a campaign of terror within the Russian Communist Party we remember as the Great Purge, culminating in the inquisitorial circus of the Moscow Show Trials two years later. It was also one he used to cement his identity as the great leader of communism, on the basis of a quite explicit policy of conflating opposition to his tyranny with attacks on notions of social justice *per se*.

In a further twist of irony, the great Stalinist bugbear Leon Trotsky invoked the same policy in crushing the revolt of Kronstadt sailors against burgeoning totalitarianism of the kind that lead eventually to Stalinism in 1921, smearing them as agents of the Tsar to reassert his own identity as a prominent member of the legitimate vanguard of the working class—even as he was shooting them "like partridges," as he phrased it at the time. This assertion of identity politics was again based on the assumption that criticism of policy and attacks on person were one and the same, and performed the same blame-shifting function.

Social democracy (and capitalist democracy more generally) does of course not tolerate quite so openly totalitarian behavior, though it likewise insists on an identity that must be obeyed irrespective of the facts. Despite having succumbed almost entirely to the autocratic and absolutist strains of neoliberalism, tested in the social laboratory of Pinochet's Chile under conditions of US-backed state terrorism, defenders of politics as usual within the context of a two-party corporate duopoly often tend reflexively to defend the process—appealing to anything up to and including the idea that having progressive politics is "divisive" and must be played down to ensure the triumph of progressive politics.

It would appear then that the authoritarian strains within the left are responsible for its proclivity for identity politics, being part of its generally unprocessed historical baggage, and give rise to its propensity to reproduce the conditions those who identify as left claim to oppose. It gives people on the left an all-too-alluring way to dispense with the onerous task of actually having to argue their politics with the unenlightened masses, who not entirely without fault see them as arrogant elitists who have better things to do than deal in facts with the uneducated.

In reducing the actual effectiveness of the left in turning it into the haughty disdain for the masses it claims to be against, identity politics on the left encourages a ghettoizing effect, which in turn feeds further contempt for the masses in the generally destructive manner of a feedback loop. The negativity of this feedback loop in turn engenders a permanent attitude of antagonism generally, which encourages in turn the "Oppression Olympics" routine, or that associated with the will to compete to be the most victimised and oppressed—not because doing actually does anything whatsoever to help in terms of overcoming victimisation and oppression, but because of the kudos to be gained within marginalized and ghettoized activists scenes where meaningful action is difficult at the best of times, and which the left makes more difficult for itself by virtue of its own general dysfunctionality. It is hardly a recipe for unity or constructive internal dialogue—a fact that appears to be borne out by the rampant, nay characteristic fracturing of the left very broadly, much less to say not a small part of the atrocious and incredibly selfish and destructive behavior that some carry on with.

At this stage, the dysfunctionality borne of identity politics within the left seems to reach its zenith. Without hope of meaningful change, the primary source of value for anyone attaching themselves to activist politics is for the kudos and social brownie points to be gained from being politically "right on," even if the work of activism itself is little more than alienated roles of permanent protest or the even drearier and alienated work of trying to convince the voting public to believe in the system as it fails them for consecutive decades on end. In this context, the level of victimization we experience becomes the source of our status within progressive political scenes, at which point it becomes incumbent to ensure that it exists permanently. Without being an exploited and oppressed worker, for example, we're all just, you know, exploited and oppressed.

As against everything described above, is the possibility for those of us of the left to engage constructively with each other and with the people around us. If means determine outcomes, as they do, then it should come a little surprised that the means that much of the left employs tends to result in the reproduction of much or all of what it professes to oppose. The continuing failure of the left to meet the offensive from the right, now manifest in the electoral triumph of the short-fingered vulgarian as well as the rise and rise of former marginal figures such as Marine Le Pen in France, is in no small part a failure to reflect on and treat its own history critically. It is also a failure to understand the opposition, which is reflected in the unwillingness of many on the left either to study the right or to engage with them, even if they are generally smug, arrogant, hateful, ignorant, toxic, obnoxious and generally unpleasant. But then again, all too often, so are we.

> "*Perspective is important, but that becomes clouded when the focus is always on claiming space rather than building communities, on erecting the perfect clubhouse rather than building broad-based movements rooted in solidarity and respect.*"

Identity Politics Is Not Working

Douglas Williams

In the following viewpoint, Douglas Williams argues that identity politics has been detrimental to current political organizing. While identity itself is crucial, identity politics has made identity into an "end rather than a means" to ensure equality. Part of identity politics involves a fetishization of certain identities, such as celebrities within movements. For Williams, real political change can take place from "broad-based movements rooted in solidarity and respect" and not organizing based on hierarchical identities that form "the perfect clubhouse." Thus substance over identity should be stressed on the political left. Williams is a dean's diversity fellow and PhD student at Wayne State University in Detroit, where he researches labor policy and working-class radical movements.

As you read, consider the following questions:

1. What does Williams mean when he states that identity politics has privileged clubhouses?
2. When does perspective become clouded, according to the viewpoint?
3. Why is it dangerous to focus on criticism, according to Williams, instead of action?

I have been involved in many organizations that fight for social justice and equality. These groups were diverse in spirit and representation. Why would they not be? Coalition work has been a part of the left since its beginning, and I always believed that any successful effort to organize the working class would have to give priority to communities that have been crushed under the heel of oppression.

It was not until I served as adviser to a queer and trans person of color group at the University of Alabama that I started questioning this outlook. We began each meeting by having attendees give an accounting of all their privileges, which felt a bit like Confessional. The few events that we would have that were open to the public (it was normally a closed group, which is why my wife, who is white, bisexual, and served as co-adviser, was not allowed to attend meetings) would always begin by telling white people in the audience to "think thrice before speaking," which kind of defeated the point of an open event. Eventually, it got to the point where even non-black queer people of color felt uncomfortable coming to meetings.

Given that the group leaders were immersed in online radical social justice circles where this type of discussion is common, this was not surprising. However, I came to some conclusions that caused me to reverse course in my thinking.

1. Identity *Politics* Is Not Working

I italicized what I did because *identity* is crucial to the human experience. It goes without saying that I, a black man who grew up in the South, experience this world differently than my wife, a white woman from the Northeast, even if we both grew up working class. Not to give these experiential differences some thought within leftist activism is to leave tools out of our toolbox when it comes to strategy, regardless of whether we are discussing policies or movement building. As Steve D'Arcy pointed out earlier this year at the Public Autonomy Project site, the way that New Left-era activists tended to flatten identity wholesale created both internal and external problems. But spend 15 minutes in most self-described "radical" activist spaces today, and you will find that leftism is now faced with the opposite problem: an increasingly Balkanized landscape where identity and representation become an end rather than a means to ensure that the spoils of an ultimate working-class victory are not distributed along the same (insert -ist and -ism here) lines as before. Perspective is important, but that becomes clouded when the focus is always on claiming space rather than building communities, on erecting the perfect clubhouse rather than building broad-based movements rooted in solidarity and respect. The former might be easy and satisfying, but the latter will actually ensure that my children grow up in a different world than I have.

2. Organizing Has Been Replaced by Posturing

The current dialogue on the social-justice left has become so thoroughly nihilistic that the prospect for ultimate victory over the systems that oppress us in ways big and small seems impossible. D'Arcy highlights this:

> The older vocabulary looked at capitalism, racism, and sexism (for example) as social systems or institutions that could and probably would be defeated, once and for all, in the foreseeable future. Accordingly, activists of that era defined and described their movements as struggles for "socialism," "black liberation,"

or "women's liberation." By contrast, the new vocabulary tends to suspend judgment on (without denying) the prospects for ultimate victory, and to focus its attention on challenging everyday impacts of capitalism, racialization and gender, in the here and now. This prioritization of resistance to everyday impacts infuses, not only the way activists today talk, but also how they choose what to do.

In such an environment, everything is turned upside down. We treat the ardent defense of millionaire celebrities as a form of radicalism. We engage in endless repetition of grievances without engaging in a discussion of better practices. We treat every ancillary skirmish like the defining battle of a war that seemingly has no end game. Or, as Adolph Reed, Jr., put it in *Harper's*,

> The left careens from this oppressed group or crisis moment to that one, from one magical or morally pristine constituency or source of political agency … to another. It lacks focus and stability; its métier is bearing witness, demonstrating solidarity, and the event or the gesture. Its reflex is to "send messages" to those in power, to make statements, and to stand with or for the oppressed.

When will we decide that we have sent enough messages and start building power? Actual power, not the power that comes from perfecting a clubhouse or meeting structure, but rather from the articulation of a vision and a plan to execute said vision? When do we start looking at the moving parts, looking out 5-10-20 years, and start piecing together a strategy to fight the forces of reaction, revanchism, and repression? It is no longer enough to simply act as a town crier, monotonously calling out every problem and grievance facing our world; it is time to act.

> *"Identity politics is not contrary to the American way; it is the American way!"*

Identity Politics Is Part of the American Experience

Ron Daniels

In the following viewpoint, Ron Daniels asserts that identity politics is integral to the American experience and has been around since the founding of America itself. While it was first used by early, white Europeans who immigrated to America for new opportunities, other groups of people began to realize the utility of identity politics in political organizing. Daniels uses the conservative response to the nomination of Supreme Court justice Sonya Sotomayor in 2009 as a launching pad to make his argument that one reason identity politics is often critiqued is because of conservative fears that different groups of people will form a "rainbow coalition" that threatens their traditional worldviews. Daniels is president of the Institute of the Black World 21st Century and distinguished lecturer at York College City University of New York.

"In Defense of 'Identity Politics,'" by Ron Daniels, Z Commentaries, June 27, 2009. Reprinted by permission.

As you read, consider the following questions:

1. How does Ron Daniels define identity politics?
2. Why does Daniels link identity politics to American identity?
3. Daniels suggests that white ethno-nationalists first used identity politics, which necessitated the use of identity politics for minorities. Does this ring true to you?

The nomination of Judge Sotomayor for Justice on the Supreme Court has simply sent some conservatives into a tizzy, searching for anything that might derail her historic quest to be the first Latina to occupy a seat on this august body. One of the allegations that has surfaced is that she is a proponent of "identity politics," the appeal to solidarity within a racial, ethnic or issue constituency to advance the interest/agenda of a particular group. Conservatives have widely disparaged such efforts as separatist, divisive and corrosive of the idea of assimilating into the American culture. Critics point to Judge Sotomayor's statement that a "wise Latina" might bring a better perspective on some issues than a White man and description of herself as an "affirmative action baby" as evidence that she is a captive of identity politics. In a recent column in the New York Times, conservative columnist David Brooks, who actually had some favorable things to say about Judge Sotomayor, suggested that she attended Princeton University when "the whole race, class and gender academic-industrial complex seemed fresh, exciting and just." He goes on to say that "there is no way she was going to get out of that unscarred." Brooks obviously subscribes to the notion that identity politics is damaging to the American way.

In my view conservatives who espouse this view are either naïve, ignorant of American history or posturing for political advantage (it could be all of the above). Identity politics is not contrary to the American way; it is the American way! With few exceptions the initial wave of intruders who sailed to these shores and dispossessed the indigenous people were White Anglo-Saxon Protestants (WASP). It is this body of Euro-ethnics along with their Scandinavian and Germanic kith and kin who established the foundations for the American culture and "identity." WASPS also captured the vital levers of power and privilege in the emerging new nation.

America was largely a WASP nation until the great migrations which occurred in response to the industrial revolution after the Civil War. Now mixed in with the Anglo-Germanic and Scandinavian people arriving on these shores were the Catholic (including Irish) and darker skinned Euro-ethnics from Southern and Eastern Europe, Italians, Greeks, Poles and other Slavic immigrants. All of these non-WASP Euro-ethnics were treated as foreigners and viewed as a threat to "American culture." They were also locked out of the centers of economic and political power. As marginalized groups, non-WASP ethnics were compelled to look inward, to use their ethnic identity, culture and religion as sources of strength in a hostile land. Their solidarity served as the foundation for internal socio-economic development and entry into the electoral political arena.

As the major political parties competed for power in local, state and national elections, organized blocs of self identified new immigrants who were once reviled and marginalized became more attractive as potential allies to achieve electoral victories. Indeed, some marginalized ethnic groups, most notably the Irish, became so adept at welding power that they became the dominant force in some of the most powerful political machines in this country, e.g., Boss Tweed in Boston, the Daley machine in Chicago and the O'Connell Machine in Albany. Marginalized groups used "identity politics" to break down the walls of social, economic and political exclusion.

For decades in most of the urban centers in the country, with the exception of the South, political parties used "ticket balancing" to make certain that every ethnic identity group was represented on their slates of candidates to improve prospects for electoral success/ victory. Over time other constituent groups like labor began to flex their muscles and therefore had to be considered as part of the electoral political equation. It is this mix of ethnic groups and issue-related interest groups that the venerable Political Scientist V. O. Keys discusses in his classic work, Politics, Parties and Pressure Groups. Identity politics is as "American as apple pie."

If White, non-WASP Euro-ethnics were forced to utilize identity politics to achieve more just and equitable treatment in their new homeland, it has been imperative that people of African descent and other people of color do likewise. Deep-seated racism/ White supremacy in America has been a formidable barrier to access to first class citizenship, equity and parity for Blacks and people of color. While it may have been difficult to distinguish between various Euro-ethnic groups because of their "whiteness," there was no hiding place for Blacks and people of color. Indeed, antagonism toward people of color has often been a source of unity among Whites despite their inter-ethnic rivalries. Consequently, racial/ethnic/cultural solidarity has been an essential element in the struggle to eradicate discrimination, segregation and exclusion from economic and political power for people of color in this country. Like their White counterparts, people of color have been compelled to utilize identity politics to demand respect, dignity, equal opportunity and democratic rights.

Based on their historical experiences as marginalized, however, Blacks and people of color are expanding the definition of the "American way" to be a more inclusive, multi-ethnic, multi-cultural, multi-religious, "empathetic," just and humane society. In this quest, they are joined by other "identity" groups like proponents of women's rights and lesbian and gay advocates. This is the real problem conservatives have with identity politics. They fear the possibility that a "Rainbow Coalition" of identity groups will pose a fundamental threat to "our cherished American way of life." And, they have every right to be fearful because "wise" representatives of Rainbow identity groups are likely to see and wish for a far different world then White men and women who are apostles of a restrictive and homogenized American identity and way of life.

> *"I believe that today's movement requires us to think and act beyond identity politics. We must create a swell of humanity who will override tribal fears and entrenched 'isms' to restore love, respect and democracy."*

The Women's March Exemplifies the Power of Identity Politics

M. J. Kaplan

In the following viewpoint, M. J. Kaplan writes about her experience in the Women's March to object Donald Trump's inauguration as US president in January 2017. She states that people took part in the Women's March despite their gender, sexual orientation, race, or ethnicity, and thus it was an inclusive and intersectional event. For Kaplan, the march exemplifies not only the power of identity politics but also the ability to move beyond simple identity politics to an intersectional and multifaceted identity politics based on political action against oppression. Kaplan is a US-based dot connector for Loomio. She also teaches at Brown University and enables charitable ventures across the globe.

As you read, consider the following questions:

1. What two events does the author contrast to open
   the viewpoint?
2. What does the author remind the reader of regarding
   marches and protests?
3. How does the march seem to both exemplify identity
   politics and signal a move beyond it?

I'd felt this power once before, 8 years ago as I arrived on the national mall with my family to wait in the freezing cold with 1.8 million others to witness the historic inauguration of Barack Obama. We felt deep pride and hopefulness that we had elected the first African American U.S. President. We were inspired by Obama's intelligence, humility and frankly his humanity. Eight years later we were awed by the integrity of the man, even though we accepted that he was unable to achieve even a small measure of our aspirations from that frigid day of celebration in 2009.

The contrast between Obama and Trump couldn't be more severe. My emotions were anger and despair when I travelled to Washington for the Women's March (still working through the stages of grief).

Before I left for D.C. I pulled out my protest paraphernalia from as far back as 1980. Reagan's election prompted my early activism. We launched a women's network to protest the escalation of nuclear power and arms. Our founder, Dr. Helen Caldicott, had successfully rallied physicians to protest the nuclear threat, leveraging her credibility as a physician to make a scientific argument. Women flocked to her talks with deep concern; however, most lacked a basic understanding of international defense policy or political organizing. So we formed WAND to educate and organize women to advocate for people-centered policies. We tapped the power dynamics of the first presidential gender gap—a distinctly partisan voting pattern between women and men that still persists. As I prepared for this Women's March 35 years later,

I was uncomfortable with gender as an organizing frame. Are we women going to save democracy from this kleptocrat? After all, 42% voting women chose Trump compared to just 54% for Clinton. And white women skewed support for Trump.

I believe that today's movement requires us to think and act beyond identity politics. We must create a swell of humanity who will override tribal fears and entrenched "isms" to restore love, respect and democracy.

The origin story of the March is a reminder that even one grassroots activist can kindle massive resistance. As I understand it, Teresa Shook, a retired attorney and grandmother of 4 living in Hawaii, created a Facebook page suggesting a protest the night after the election. The next morning more than 10,000 people had responded. Simultaneously, Bob Bland from Brooklyn proposed a protest. She had several thousand Facebook followers from the "Nasty Woman" t-shirts she produced to raise money for Planned Parenthood. They joined forces and The Women's March was born. These two women were repulsed by Trump's treatment of women and his disrespectful rhetoric. In shock from the election, their instinct was to protect their deepest concern—women's rights. So they organized their women "friends" to take to the streets to resist oppression. Social media ignited the masses.

There was plenty of in-fighting about race and gender, power and inclusion during preparations for the March as would be expected for a decentralized political movement. However, I did not experience any fracture at the March. Every aspect of the day celebrated inclusion and shared purpose. There was no police presence or violence. When a woman in a wheelchair needed to pass, the dense wall of marchers parted like the Red Sea. Children were offered perches for better visibility and men of all ages were embraced as valued allies. The theme that framed the gathering was intersectionality, a concept that originated with feminism. The March platform expressed these unity principles, "gender justice is racial justice is economic justice." I have little doubt that people are organizing through a new prism that transcends identity politics in pursuit of the power we gain as a united front.

But the March was just a beginning warns Zeynep Tufekci, an academic who writes about technology, politics and society. Tufekci writes,

> protests should be seen not as the culmination of an organizing effort, but as a first, potential step... The significance of a protest depends on what happens afterward.

Trump awakened a sleeping giant, and I don't mean the people who voted for him. Now what? The hard work has begun. The population at large rejects this administration's tyranny. The question is, can we organize effectively and leverage our power to stop this insanity? Early indications are promising. Thousands of groups are springing up across the U.S. on a daily basis. More than one million people downloaded the Indivisible Guide produced by progressive congressional staffers to teach people how to influence Congress. RISE is another new citizen watchdog group gaining traction. And of course there are thousands of existing groups such as 350.org that already have engaged networks.

In my home of Providence, Rhode Island, the smallest and one of the bluest states, 1000 neighbours gathered the Saturday after the election to organize. Actions are continuing on a regular basis. Last Sunday, over 1000 people again rallied at our State House to decry the White House ban on people entering the U.S. from several Muslim countries. Even though we have a democratic congressional delegation, our Senators were flooded by rebukes when they approved Mike Pompeo's appointment as Director of the CIA. After the immigration rally, protesters marched to a community dinner sponsored by Senator Whitehouse. Few could enter the crowded building so the Senator came outside to talk with the crowd. He later thanked those who had waited outside in the cold after the auditorium reached capacity. "I want you to know I heard all of your voices clearly, and I share your outrage about what we've seen from President Trump this week," Whitehouse wrote. "There are going to be big fights ahead, and we're going to have to keep speaking up and standing together. It has rarely mattered more."

This is democracy in action.

Organizing takes place in groups big and small collaborating online and in person. They are place-based and issue focused and teeming with first time activists and old-timers alike. People are convening in person to share their fears and hopes, to strategize and to meditate. They're also are capitalizing on technology to act fast to thwart threats. Digital organizing tools help mobilize distributed networks. Tufekci notes that we can learn from the Tea Party protests of 2009 that also mobilized thousands of protesters with the help of digital communications. Tea Party protesters pursued a "ferociously focused agenda" according to Tufekci. They identified and supported "primary candidates to challenge Republicans who did not agree with their demands, keeping close tabs on legislation and pressuring politicians who deviated from a Tea Party platform." We must be intersectional, focused, sophisticated and agile to combat this regime.

In a provocative article in The Atlantic, David Frum writes,

> Those citizens who fantasize about defying tyranny from within fortified compounds have never understood how liberty is actually threatened in a modern bureaucratic state: not by diktat and violence, but by the slow, demoralizing process of corruption and deceit. And the way that liberty must be defended is not with amateur firearms, but with an unwearying insistence upon the honesty, integrity, and professionalism of American institutions and those who lead them. We are living through the most dangerous challenge to the free government of the United States that anyone alive has encountered. What happens next is up to you and me. Don't be afraid. This moment of danger can also be your finest hour as a citizen and an American.

Let this be our finest hour as citizens of the world.

> "*Identity politics hinges on perceptible racial or ethnic solidarity, but citizens are increasingly a mixture of various races and do not always categorize themselves as 'non-white.'*"

The End of Identity Politics Is Near

Victor Davis Hanson

In the following viewpoint, Victor Davis Hanson focuses on the historical roles that identity politics has played, which has included initiating devastating wars. However, the time has come, according to the author, for identity politics to die out. This may not be a conscious effort to change strategy on the part of political organizers but rather because of biological changes. As the world is becoming more interconnected and different ethnicities are mixing together, it will be hard to distinguish between groups of people based on race or ethnicity. For Hanson, then, the vociferous claims of "diversity" advocates are because they know they are losing their claim to fixed and recognizable ethnic and racial identities. Hanson is the Martin and Illie Anderson senior fellow at the Hoover Institution; his focus is classics and military history.

"The End Of Identity Politics," by Victor Davis Hanson, The Board of Trustees of Leland Stanford Junior University, February 17, 2017. Reprinted by permission.

As you read, consider the following questions:

1. Who are so-called "hyphenated Americans"?
2. What does the author mean by a "diversity industry?"
3. What has emerged as a better barometer of privilege than race in America, according to the viewpoint?

Who are we? asked the liberal social scientist Samuel Huntington over a decade ago in a well-reasoned but controversial book. Huntington feared the institutionalization of what Theodore Roosevelt a century earlier had called "hyphenated Americans." A "hyphenated American," Roosevelt scoffed, "is not an American at all." And 30 years ago, another progressive stalwart and American historian Arthur Schlesinger argued in his book *The Disuniting of America* that identity politics were tearing apart the cohesion of the United States.

What alarmed these liberals was the long and unhappy history of racial, religious, and ethnic chauvinism, and how such tribal ties could prove far stronger than shared class affinities. Most important, they were aware that identity politics had never proved to be a stabilizing influence on any past multiracial society. Indeed, most wars of the 20th century and associated genocides had originated over racial and ethnic triumphalism, often by breakaway movements that asserted tribal separateness. Examples include the Serbian and Slavic nationalist movements in 1914 against Austria-Hungary, Hitler's rise to power on the promise of German ethno-superiority, the tribal bloodletting in Rwanda, and the Shiite/Sunni/Kurdish conflicts in Iraq.

The United States could have gone the way of these other nations. Yet, it is one of the few successful multiracial societies in history. America has survived slavery, civil war, the Japanese-American internment, and Jim Crow—and largely because it has upheld three principles for unifying, rather than dividing, individuals.

The first concerns the Declaration of Independence and the American Constitution, which were unique documents for

their time and proved transcendent across time and space. Both
documents enshrined the ideal that all people were created equal
and were human first, with inalienable rights from God that
were protected by government. These founding principles would
eventually trump innate tribal biases and prejudices to grant all
citizens their basic rights.

Second, given America's two-ocean buffer, the United States
could control its own demographic destiny. Americans usually
supported liberal immigration policies largely because of the
country's ability to monitor the numbers of new arrivals and
the melting pot's ability to assimilate, integrate, and intermarry
immigrants, who would soon relegate their racial, religious, and
ethnic affinities to secondary importance.

Finally, the United States is the most individualistic and
capitalistic of the Western democracies. The nation was blessed
with robust economic growth, rich natural resources, and plenty
of space. It assumed that its limited government and ethos of
entrepreneurialism would create enough widespread prosperity
and upward mobility that affluence—or at least the shared quest
for it—would create a common bond superseding superficial Old
World ties based on appearance or creed.

In the late 1960s, however, these three principles took a hit. The
federal government lost confidence in the notion that civil rights
legislation, the melting pot, and a growing economy could unite
Americans and move society in the direction of Martin Luther
King Jr.'s vision—"I have a dream that my four little children will
one day live in a nation where they will not be judged by the color
of their skin, but by the content of their character."

This shift from the ideal of the melting pot to the triumph of
salad-bowl separatism occurred, in part, because the Democratic
Party found electoral resonance in big government's generous
entitlements and social programs tailored to particular groups.
By then, immigration into the United States had radically shifted
and become less diverse. Rather than including states in Europe
and the former British Commonwealth, most immigrants were

poorer and almost exclusively hailed from the nations of Latin America, Asia, and Africa, resulting in poorer immigrants who, upon arrival, needed more government help. Another reason for the shift was the general protest culture of the Vietnam era, which led to radical changes in everything from environmental policy to sexual identity, and thus saw identity politics as another grievance against the status quo.

A half-century later, affirmative action and identity politics have created a huge diversity industry, in which millions in government, universities, and the private sector are entrusted with teaching the values of the Other and administering de facto quotas in hiring and admissions. In 2016, Hillary Clinton ran a campaign on identity politics, banking on the notion that she could reassemble various slices of the American electorate, in the fashion that Barack Obama had in 2008 and 2012, to win a majority of voters. She succeeded, as did Obama, in winning the popular vote by appealing directly to the unique identities of gays, Muslims, feminists, blacks, Latinos, and an array of other groups, but misjudged the Electoral College and so learned that a numerical majority of disparate groups does not always translate into winning key swing states.

At one point Clinton defined her notion of identity politics by describing Trump's supporters: "You know, to just be grossly generalistic, you could put half of Trump's supporters into what I call the basket of deplorables. Right? The racist, sexist, homophobic, xenophobic, Islamaphobic—you name it. And unfortunately there are people like that. And he has lifted them up... Now, some of those folks—they are irredeemable, but thankfully they are not America."

What is the future of diversity politics after the 2016 election? Uncertain at best—and for a variety of reasons.

One, intermarriage and integration are still common. Overall, about 15 percent of all marriages each year are interracial, and the rates are highest for Asians and Latinos. Forty percent of Asian women marry men of another race—one quarter of African-American males do, as well—and over a quarter of all Latinos marry someone non-Latino.

IDENTITY POLITICS IN PRESIDENTIAL ELECTIONS

Are American voters still suckers for identity politics? Have they not learned that character matters more to leadership than some random physical trait, say: race, color, or creed? Did Franklin Delano Roosevelt's race help him win World War II? Did Ronald Reagan's creed help him win the Cold War? What was his creed?

Americans fell for identity politics in 2008 when they elected Barack Obama, at least in part because he could lay claim to being African-American. Even I was rather glad when he won. Now maybe all the claptrap about America being a racist country might subside. Let the Germans and French catch up with America. Of course, my enthusiasm for Mr. Obama evanesced a bit when the economy continued to fizzle and our foreign policy began to make it downright dangerous to carry an American passport in some parts of the world. Now with the economy slipping back toward recession and a ragtag army committing atrocities in the Middle East that have not been practiced by armies since the Dark Ages, even as our President polishes up his golf game, I am looking to elect a leader to the White House in 2016 not a community activist or even a gifted mesmerist.

Yet I hear murmurings that 2016 is the time for America's first woman president. That woman is not for a certitude the Republican, Carly Fiorina, though she has—without benefit of money or staff—waged a terrific early campaign, asking all the right questions, displaying poise, acuity, and an agile mind. Moreover her questions are directed at the right target, the duplicitous, money-grubbing Hillary Clinton. Does anyone doubt that Ms. Fiorina has the courage, the energy, and the grasp of the issues to make Clinton cry out to rid her of this Republican woman?

How long are our elections going to revolve around the questions of gender or race or humble birth? When will we return to asking the most important questions of whether our candidates are sufficiently fortified by good character to make the right decisions and govern wisely? Frankly it has been an embarrassingly long time since a candidate's character or lack thereof mattered in an American presidential election.

"The Future of Identity Politics," Spectator.org, June 3, 2015.

Identity politics hinges on perceptible racial or ethnic solidarity, but citizens are increasingly a mixture of various races and do not always categorize themselves as "non-white." Without DNA badges, it will be increasingly problematic to keep racial pedigrees straight. And sometimes the efforts to do so reach the point of caricature and inauthenticity, through exaggerated accent marks, verbal trills, voice modulations, and nomenclature hyphenation. One reason why diversity activists sound shrill is their fear that homogenization is unrelenting.

Second, the notion of even an identifiable and politically monolithic group of non-white minorities is also increasingly suspect. Cubans do not have enough in common with Mexicans to advance a united Latino front. African-Americans are suspicious of open borders that undercut entry-level job wages. Asians resent university quotas that often discount superb grades and test scores to ensure racial diversity. It is not clear that Hmong-Americans have much in common with Japanese-Americans, or that Punjabi immigrants see themselves politically akin to Chinese newcomers as fellow Asians.

Third, ethnic solidarity can cut both ways. In the 2016 elections, Trump won an overwhelming and nearly unprecedented number of working class whites in critical swing states. Many either had not voted in prior elections or had voted Democratic. The culture's obsession with tribalism and special ethnic interests—often couched in terms of opposing "white privilege"—had alienated millions of less well-off white voters. Quietly, many thought that if ethnic activists were right that the white majority was shrinking into irrelevance, and if it was acceptable for everyone to seek solidarity through their tribal affiliations, then poor whites could also rally under the banner of their own identity politics. If such trends were to continue in a nation that is still 70 percent white, it would prove disastrous for the Democratic Party in a way never envisioned during the era of Barack Obama. Hillary Clinton discovered that Obama's identity politics constituencies were not transferrable to herself in the same exceptional numbers, and the effort to ensure that they were often created new tribal opponents.

Fourth, it is not certain that immigration, both legal and illegal, will continue at its current near record rate, which has resulted in over 40 million immigrants now residing in America—constituting some 13 percent of the present population. Trump is likely not just to curtail illegal immigration, but also to return legal immigration to a more meritocratic, diverse, and individual basis. Were immigration to slow down and become more diverse, the formidable powers of integration and intermarriage would perhaps do to the La Raza community what it once did to the Italian-American minority after the cessation of mass immigration from Italy. There are currently no Italian-American quotas, no Italian university departments, and no predictable voting blocs.

Fifth, class is finally reemerging as a better barometer of privilege than is race—a point that Republican populists are starting to hammer home. The children of Barack Obama, for example, have far more privilege than do the sons of Appalachian coal miners—and many Asian groups already exceed American per capita income averages. When activist Michael Eric Dyson calls for blanket reparations for slavery, his argument does not resonate with an unemployed working-class youth from Kentucky, who was born more than 30 years after the emergence of affirmative action—and enjoys a fraction of Dyson's own income, net worth, and cultural opportunities.

Finally, ideology is eroding the diversity industry. Conservative minorities and women are not considered genuine voices of the Other, given their incorrect politics. For all its emphasis on appearance, diversity is really an intolerant ideological movement that subordinates race and gender to progressive politics. It is not biology that gives authenticity to feminism, but leftwing assertions; African-American conservatives are often derided as inauthentic, not because of purported mixed racial pedigrees, but due to their unorthodox beliefs.

The 2016 election marked an earthquake in the diversity industry. It is increasingly difficult to judge who we are merely by our appearances, which means that identity politics may lose its influence. These fissures probably explain some of the ferocity of the protests we've seen in recent weeks. A dying lobby is fighting to hold on to its power.

> *"Identity politics hinges on perceptible racial or ethnic solidarity, but citizens are increasingly a mixture of various races and do not always categorize themselves as 'non-white.'"*

A Political Revolution Is Coming

Michael Lind

In the following viewpoint, Michael Lind states that a revolution is at hand where traditional concepts like "left," "right," and "center" will be overturned. While "God, gays, and guns" and other social issues will no longer interest millennial voters, they will focus more and more on economic concerns. Out of this realignment will emerge two broad political movements, according to Lind, the liberaltarians (including libertarians who favor less government involvement) and the populiberals (social liberals who favor larger government). These two movements will be focused in, respectively, downtown cities and suburbia, thus creating an identity politics focused less on "who Americans are but where they live." Lind is a cofounder of the New America Foundation and author of Land of Promise: An Economic History of the United States.

"The Coming Realignment: Cities, Class, and Ideology After Social Conservatism," by Michael Lind, The Breakthrough Institute, April 28, 2014. Reprinted by permission.

As you read, consider the following questions:

1. What percentage of millennials identify as liberal, according to the 2009 poll cited in the viewpoint?
2. What classification does the author propose instead of the traditional left-right spectrum?
3. What are Densitaria and Posturbia, according to the viewpoint?

God, gays, and guns. The era in which controversies over so-called social issues like these defined the Right and the Left in American politics is rapidly coming to an end, thanks to the pronounced liberalism of the youngest cohort of Americans—the Millennial generation, whose members were born in 1981 or later.

God? Millennials are the least religious of Americans. A quarter are "nones" or unaffiliated, according to a Gospel Coalition poll, and fewer than one in ten say that religion is important in their lives.[1]

Guns? According to a Gallup poll, fewer Americans between the ages of 18 and 29 own guns (20 percent) than the national average (30 percent).[2] And a majority of Millennials support gun control: 56 percent, according to a National Journal poll,[3] and 59 percent, according to Pew.[4]

Gays? According to a Pew poll, the Millennials are the only cohort in which a majority (70 percent) support gay marriage.[5]

Millennials are also more likely than members of older generations to describe themselves as liberal, according to a 2009 Pew poll: 29 percent, compared to 40 percent moderate and 28 percent conservative.[6] Only 20 percent of members of Generation X, 18 percent of Baby Boomers, and 15 percent of members of the Silent Generation describe themselves as liberal.[7] While individuals often become somewhat more conservative as they grow older, it seems likely that the Millennial generation will permanently shift American attitudes to the left—on social issues, if not necessarily on economics.

Thanks to generational shifts in values like these, it is likely that in the decades ahead there will be a dramatic realignment in American politics. Although it is likely to reshape the two major parties, it will not be a mere "partisan realignment" of the kind studied by political scientists. Rather, it will be a realignment of American public philosophies or political worldviews. This worldview realignment will be accentuated by a number of long-term demographic and cultural changes. But the chief catalyst of the realignment will be the near-universal victory of social liberalism. In a nation in which both parties are socially liberal, existing coalitions are likely to break up and reform in striking ways.

1.

My argument begins with the familiar observation that Americans today are divided about social issues like gay rights and abortion as well as about economic issues like inequality, taxes, wages, and trade. These cross-cutting and overlapping disagreements produce a pattern of political worldviews that is more complex than a simple Left–Right political spectrum. A closer approximation to reality is provided by a four-square grid, in which one axis represents support for social liberalism and the other support for economic libertarianism, defined as antigovernment and pro-market attitudes. (In the rest of the world, "liberalism" is used to mean the anti-statist, pro-market alternative to "social democracy" or "progressivism," but in the United States, "social democracy," "progressivism," and "liberalism" are often used as synonyms; to avoid confusion I use the term "libertarianism" for opposition to a large role for the state in the economic realm, and the term "liberalism" for support for an active and generous government.)

When political and economic attitudes are correlated in this way, four worldviews result:

- Liberalism: social liberalism combined with economic liberalism.

- Conservatism: economic libertarianism with state enforcement of conservative values in the social realm (for example, laws against abortion and sodomy).
- Libertarianism: anti-statism in both the social and economic realms.
- Populism: a combination of economic liberalism and social conservatism.

If the United States used a version of proportional representation, the electoral system that is used by most other modern democracies, it might have a multiparty system in which most or all of those worldviews were represented. In Germany, for example, the Social Democrats have traditionally occupied what I am calling the consistent liberal position; the Christian Democrats are close to American populists in their combination of moderately conservative social values with support for a welfare state and "social market economy"; and there is even a moderately libertarian party, the Free Democrats. But the first-past-the-post plurality electoral system inherited by the U.S. from Britain, which penalizes third parties, tends to ensure that two major parties will always exist, imposed on a population that is not divided along simply binary lines.

As a result, American parties are coalitions, not merely of interest groups, but also of what might be called worldview groups. So are broad American political movements. The American Left has long included a dwindling number of socially conservative working-class union members as well as socially liberal upper-middle-class reformers. Similarly, the contemporary American Right is divided between a white working-class populist base suspicious of Wall Street and a libertarian political class funded by Wall Street and serving its interests.

During the last quarter of the twentieth century, white working-class populists were the most important swing vote in American politics. Alienated by the Civil Rights revolution and the adoption of social liberalism by Democratic leaders and activists during and after the 1960s, many former Democratic voters retained their support for middle-class social insurance programs like Social Security and Medicare and distrusted the Republican Party, which was identified too closely with the rich, business, and finance.

The only two-term presidents of this period, Ronald Reagan and Bill Clinton, succeeded in electoral terms by playing to the values of non-Hispanic white populist swing voters. Reagan exploited the white working-class animus toward socially liberal elites and the welfare-dependent poor, while quietly dropping his early plans to cut or dismantle Social Security and other programs popular with the white working class. With equal success, Clinton did the reverse, distancing himself from social liberals in his party by symbolic stances including support for police and "law and order," support of the death penalty, opposition to gay marriage and to military service by openly gay soldiers, and a well-calculated attack on Sister Souljah, a black rapper who rhetorically wondered: "If Black people kill Black people every day, why not have a week and kill white people?"[8]

Populist Reagan Democrats were not the only group alienated from both parties in late twentieth-century America. A substantial minority of consistent libertarians supported social liberalism and moderate libertarian economic policies, such as deregulation, smaller government, and free trade and immigration. They were found in both the libertarian wing of the GOP and the neoliberal wing of the Democrats. But while their base among the rich and upper-middle-class professionals gave them influence far out of proportion to their numbers, they lacked the numbers to be important swing voters on the scale of the blue-collar Reagan Democrats.

2.

This post-1960s pattern of crisscross alliances and appeals among liberals, conservatives, populists, and libertarians is likely to be radically simplified, as a result of the triumph of social liberalism in the American electorate.

Younger generations are increasingly liberal and secular on social issues compared with their older counterparts. On social issues, nearly three in four Millennials now support same-sex marriage.[9] Millennials are more likely to view the increasing numbers of interracial relationships and women in the workforce as positive changes and are less concerned about the rise of unmarried parents.[10] In a reversal from 1990s attitudes, more young women than young men say that being professionally successful is very important in their lives.[11]

Increasing liberalism in social values is associated with declining religious belief and affiliation. While Americans remain more religious than most people in other developed nations,[12] the pace of secularization in the U.S. is striking. According to the Pew Forum on Religion and Public Life,[13] in 2012 just under 20 percent of Americans claimed no religious affiliation, an increase of 5 percentage points in only five years. While a majority of the unaffiliated claim to believe in God, 6 percent of Americans describe themselves as atheists and agnostics. Among adults under 30, one-third have no religious affiliation, compared to one-fifth in the population as a whole. The most recent General Social Survey found that 26 percent of people ages 18 to 30—the Millennials—had no affiliation with a particular religion.[14] If it were a denomination, the unaffiliated group would be the fastest growing "religion" in America.[15] It is possible that Millennials might become somewhat more religious as they age.[16] But it is more likely that the U.S. is simply a laggard in a global trend toward secularization in advanced industrial societies that is more mature in the increasingly post-Christian societies of Europe.

Taken together, these trends augur the disappearance of two of the squares in the imaginary four-square grid built from interacting social and economic attitudes. The two positions that are likely to dwindle in importance, if not disappear altogether, are the two positions that are characterized by conservative views on social issues: populism and conservatism. In an America in which the electorate shares a consensus on social liberalism, only two major political worldviews would remain: liberalism (social liberalism combined with support for large, activist government) and libertarianism (social liberalism combined with opposition to large, activist government).

The replacement of four broad political worldviews by two, thanks to the collapse of social conservatism, will lead to changes in political terminology and alterations in major-party voting patterns that will be surprising and unforeseen. But some predictions can be ventured.

To begin with, the terms "liberal" or "progressive" and "conservative" are likely to have quite different meanings a generation from now. These terms change their meaning every generation or two. In the early 1950s, American conservatives supported protectionism and isolationism. By the 1980s, American conservatism stood for free trade and a hawkish foreign policy.

The tendency in popular discourse to classify movements and parties as being on the left or the right originated in the seating arrangements of the revolutionary French national assembly in the eighteenth century and will probably persist. If the major division in American politics a generation from now pits what today would be called liberals against what today would be called libertarians, it is likely that the terms "Left" and "Right" will be assigned to those two broad schools of thought. But as I will argue, it might be a mistake to equate libertarian, Right, and Republican; or progovernment, Left, and Democrat.

For the purposes of this discussion, and to avoid premature assignment of emerging worldviews to the left or the right, I propose to call the two broad political movements that I am predicting *liberaltarians* and *populiberals*.

The term liberaltarian is already in use, to describe a broad camp including neoliberal Democrats skeptical of government in the economic sphere along with libertarian Republicans and independents who recognize the need for more government than libertarian ideologues believe to be legitimate.

Populiberal is my own coinage. It describes social liberals who share the liberal social values of liberaltarians, but who tend to be more egalitarian and to favor a greater role for the government in matters like social insurance, business-labor relations, and redistribution of income. Populiberal parties in this sense would include the socially liberal members of parties or movements that are considered to be on the right in other democracies, such as German Christian Democrats or French Gaullists who support legal abortion and gay rights.

3.

Until this point, this discussion has focused on abstract ideology. It is time to provide more context to the picture I am painting, by incorporating more demographic and geographic detail.

The contested terrain between economic issues and social issues is often the home of lifestyle politics and identity politics. Both will continue to exist in some form, even if most Americans eventually adopt progressive positions on issues involving sex and reproduction or the relationship between church and state. Indeed, even if some kinds of identity politics, based on racial polarization and religious disputes, fade in political importance over time, new conflicts will emerge. Differences of interest and value in economic matters are likely to be expressed indirectly through a new politics of lifestyle and identity based less on who Americans are than on where they live.

Following the convention that assigns the color red to signify Republican electoral victories and blue to the Democratic Party, Americans have fallen into the habit of talking about "red states" and "blue states" or even "red America" and "blue America." But an examination of results in presidential and congressional elections at the level of counties or congressional districts produces a much more kaleidoscopic map, in which Democratic-leaning blue urban areas tend to be surrounded by Republican-leaning red suburbs, exurbs, and rural regions.[17] While historic differences among regions like the South and New England continue to shape politics, this distinction within states rather than among them may be a clue to the future of American politics.

In the next generation, we may see the continuing emergence of two societies on American soil, with quite different patterns of class structure, economic organization, and government. At the risk of burdening readers with too many neologisms, I propose calling these societies Densitaria and Posturbia. Densitaria is the natural political-geographic base of liberaltarianism, just as Posturbia is the natural political-geographic base of populiberalism.

By Densitaria I mean high-density downtowns of major cities, as well as high-density business and residential sectors spread throughout broader metropolitan areas. As urban experts like Joel Kotkin have pointed out, what I am calling Densitaria is the next stage in the continuing evolution of urban areas in the U.S. and similar advanced industrial societies.[18] In the twentieth century, thanks to trucking and the electric grid, factory production migrated out of downtowns to low-cost suburbs or exurbs or foreign countries. Business headquarters and high-end financial and business services remained, clustered in the urban core. Corporate and foundation headquarters will remain downtown in major cities like New York and San Francisco and Washington, D.C. But as much of their clerical labor is displaced by automation, outsourcing, or offshoring, the headquarters buildings are losing much of their practical function and are becoming trophies for executives and shareholders. In cities like New York and San Francisco, the older mixed economy is giving way to a *plutonomy*, to use a term coined by Ajay Kapur—an economy characterized by high-end luxury goods and services.[19]

As the working class and many middle-class professionals abandon Densitaria for the cheaper housing and office parks of Posturbia, the high-density downtowns and suburban villages are coming to have an hourglass-shaped social structure, with wealthy individuals at the top, many of them rentiers living off their investments, and a large luxury-service proletariat at the bottom. Increasingly, the service proletariat in Densitarian areas in the U.S., and also in Europe, is foreign-born.

Geographic variations in inequality are familiar in the U.S. today, of course. According to 2012 U.S. Census data, the most equal states during the period 2008-2012 were Alaska, Utah, Wyoming,

New Hampshire, Idaho, Hawaii, and Iowa. At the other extreme, the most unequal states during the same period were the District of Columbia, New York, Connecticut, Louisiana, Mississippi, Florida, and California.[20] The states that win their dubious prizes in the inequality sweepstakes do so thanks largely to particular Densitarian urban regions—the D.C. metro area, the greater New York region, the San Francisco Bay Area, and Los Angeles.

With its combination of economic libertarianism and social liberalism, liberaltarianism as a public philosophy appeals to the Densitarian rich, including many Democratic members of urban economic elites. Liberaltarianism justifies not only their values, like support for legal abortion and same-sex marriage, but also their interests, like the low taxes on capital gains that benefit so many in the investor class.

Liberaltarianism is not libertarianism. It is compatible with support for some kind of welfare state. But the hourglass class system of Densitaria argues for a means-tested safety net, rather than universal, middle-class social insurance.

Traditional universal social insurance, like Social Security and Medicare, chiefly benefits the middle class defined as the median class (including most of what is called the working class in other countries). In return, the broad middle class is the chief source of funding for social insurance, by means of universal, flat payroll taxes or similar universal levies. Most welfare transfers are from working-age members of the broad middle to members of their own class who cannot work—because they are old, young, sick, disabled, or temporarily unemployed. The universal middle-class version of the welfare state is solidarity, not charity.

In highly unequal societies—like many Latin American countries, or cities like New York and San Francisco—the middle of the metaphorical hourglass is squeezed between the rich and the poor. In such a social order, the argument for means-testing the welfare state, eliminating negligible benefits for the rich in order to somewhat expand benefits for the poor, may seem to be more persuasive.

The opposite logic holds in the low-density, low-rent environment of Posturbia, consisting of residential neighborhoods that are dominated by single-family housing and decentralized office parks, malls, and stores. Because the rich, in America as elsewhere, prefer to congregate in expensive, fashionable urban neighborhoods, there will be relatively few rich people in Posturbia. At the same time, the pattern of single-family housing has the effect of excluding people who are too poor to own homes rather than rent.

For these reasons, the emergent society of Posturbia is much more egalitarian than that of Densitaria, by default more than by design. While Densitarian urban areas have an hourglass social structure, the Posturbian suburbs, exurbs, and small towns tend to have a diamond-shaped class system, with few rich, few poor, and a dominant middle. In this environment, universal social insurance—based on the bargain that everybody works, everybody pays, and everybody benefits—can be expected to seem more practical and to win more political support than in the hierarchical Densitarian downtowns.

Another fault line in national politics will be federal tax policy. Posturbian populiberals might seek to tax the liberaltarian rich of Densitaria to pay for universal social insurance and public services for the working class. Conversely, the liberaltarian elite might seek to force Posturbia to shoulder the burdens of paying for their servants among the local Densitarian poor and bailing out the Densitarian rich (for example, by means of federal bailouts like TARP).

The populiberals of Posturbia and the liberaltarians of Densitaria are likely to disagree as well as on the question of the "nanny state"—that is, the legitimacy of efforts by government to manipulate the behavior of citizens for their own benefit. The nanny state is the natural corollary of the means-tested welfare state. If, by being means-tested, the welfare state turns from a system of transfers within the broad middle class into a kind of government-mediated charity or philanthropy, in which the rich are taxed to provide a safety net for the poor, the rich are likely to insist that the poor be persuaded or compelled to avoid behaviors that drive up the costs of their lifestyle mistakes to the government. Consider billionaire New York City mayor Michael Bloomberg's campaign to reduce obesity among the urban poor. His use of methods like banning large-size soft drinks[21] is a perfect example of liberaltarian behavioral cost containment, presented as altruism.

Populiberals might agree with liberaltarian champions of the nanny state with respect to many goals, like promoting healthy behavior. But they are likely to be wary of attempts at top-down social and moral engineering by economic and political elites. One response might be a populist "don't tread on me" attitude toward public attempts to micromanage individual behavior in the name of the individual's own good, whether by conditions on social insurance or tax-based nudges. Transposed to behavioral regulation, the universalist logic of populiberalism would support direct, black-letter regulation by means of laws or ordinances over elite attempts at subtle manipulation of the behavior of citizens.

The split between Posturbia and Densitaria may be most apparent with regard to environmental issues and identities. The property-owning majorities of Posturbia are likely to be more sensitive to restrictions on what property owners can do with their property than the majorities in Densitarian downtowns and edge cities, in which not only the working poor and the working class but also many professionals must rent because they cannot afford to buy a home. With much of the economy of Densitaria drawn from rents from finance, insurance, and real estate (FIRE) industries, local elites can favor stringent environmental regulations at little cost to their own paper-based, white collar industries and incomes. In contrast, most productive economic activities, including manufacturing, agriculture, and mining, including fossil fuel extraction, will occur far from upscale downtowns and neighborhoods; and the communities that view these activities as a source of local prosperity are more likely to weigh the costs as well as the benefits of environmental policies.

The evolving Posturbian populiberal coalition will likely take a different view of energy production and climate change than the Densitarian liberaltarian coalition. The environmental agenda of liberaltarian Densitaria has mostly driven Democratic climate and energy policy in recent decades, characterized by complex pollution trading schemes that would benefit the financial sector, energy taxes that would disproportionately hurt the industrial sectors of Posturbia, efforts to halt energy projects like the Keystone XL pipeline, Keynesian energy retrofitting programs for the urban poor, and subsidized solar panels for the wealthy.

A populiberal coalition that favored mitigation of global warming might offer very different climate and energy policies than the liberaltarian solutions that dominate debate today, embracing expanded gas and nuclear energy production to meet the demands of Posturbia's more energy intensive economic base while reducing air pollution and carbon emissions. Already, a boom in natural gas fracking has resulted in an annual $100 billion stimulus to the economy in the form of lower energy prices since 2007, as well as hundreds of thousands of new working-class jobs,[22] mostly in Posturbia. In the process gas has displaced coal in the nation's energy mix, reducing air pollution and carbon emissions.[23]

Such a realignment might not necessarily end up on the Republican side of the ledger. The fracking boom in swing states like Ohio helped re-elect President Obama in 2012.[24] In a major climate speech in the summer of 2013, Obama further embraced the fracking boom as an explicit strategy to address climate change,[25] breaking with his Party's Densitarian wing. Many Posturbian Democrats have broken with the Party's Densitarian wing over the Keystone XL pipeline.

Cap and trade legislation, conversely, went down to ignominious defeat in the face of opposition in the Senate from populiberal Democrats like Sherrod Brown from Ohio,[26] while a growing number of prominent Republicans, most of them out of office, have embraced modest carbon pricing in exchange for regressive tax cuts as part of a broad push for tax reform.

4.

My argument is that, as a result of spreading social liberalism, in the realm of public philosophy today's divisions among liberals, conservatives, populists, and libertarians will gradually be simplified into a binary division among liberaltarians and populiberals who share social liberalism but disagree on other things. Each of these worldviews, moreover, is likely to have a home address—the income-stratified communities of Densitaria, in the case of liberaltarianism, and the less unequal communities of Posturbia, in the case of populiberalism.

To be sure, other factors—ethnic, regional, economic, religious—will complicate this picture. And the two major political parties will continue to be coalitions of other groups in the electorate and the donor class, at the price of inconsistency.

Nevertheless, it seems safe to predict that, if American attitudes evolve along the lines that I have suggested, liberaltarians will be more concentrated in one party and populiberals more concentrated in its rival. Which public philosophy is likely to dominate which party? Different scenarios can be imagined.

In one scenario, the Republican Party would be primarily identified with liberaltarianism. This would not be the result of a purge of social conservatives by social liberals, of the kind that is sometimes discussed today. Remember, my premise is that in a generation or two an overwhelming majority of Americans will share attitudes that are considered socially liberal today, on matters of sex, reproduction, and the separation of church and state. Both parties are likely to adopt social liberalism.

Rather, in the scenario I am discussing, in which social liberalism has been adopted by all influential wings of the GOP, the liberaltarian wing would defeat the populiberal wing. Republican liberaltarians would abandon the extreme-libertarian goal of abolishing the welfare state by privatizing it. But their anti-statism and opposition to higher taxes would lead them to support a cheaper, means-tested liberaltarian safety net for the poor over a universalist social insurance system for the middle-class majority.

The triumph of low-tax, means-testing liberaltarians in the Republican Party could drive many non-Hispanic white working-class and middle-class voters into a Democratic Party that stood for universal benefits paid for by higher taxes. To the extent that they no longer shared the racial prejudices and conservative views on sex and reproduction of their populist "Reagan Democrat" parents or grandparents, these members of the white working class would be straightforward liberals, sharing a common, mostly economic agenda with the majority of blacks and Latinos. Downscale whites might become part of the base of a Populiberal Democratic Party, as they have not been since the New Deal/Great Society era.

But another scenario is possible. In the second scenario, the trend toward the identification of the Democrats with the economic elites of Wall Street and the FIRE sector, which began with Clinton and has continued to some degree under Obama, would make the Democrats the liberaltarian party. Even more than at present, the Democrats would be the party of Densitarian populations—the downtown and edge city elites and their supporting staff of disproportionately foreign-born, low-wage service workers.

In this scenario, the Republicans would become the Populiberal party of Posturbia. By dropping the coded racist appeals that have been used by Republican politicians since the backlash against the Civil Rights revolution, the GOP might attempt to join blacks and Latinos to a more socially liberal, white working-class base.

But a populiberal Republican Party, based among the multiracial working class and middle class of low-density areas, would need to abandon economic libertarianism, in favor of support for a universalist welfare state instead of a means-tested safety net. The intellectuals, politicians, and donors on the right for whom the holy grail is the destruction of middle-class entitlements like Social Security and Medicare would need to be marginalized in the Republican Party or driven to a more liberaltarian Democratic Party, which embraced means-testing even as the GOP abandoned it.

If I am right, then those who predict a permanent Democratic majority based on the relative growth of the nonwhite population may be wrong. At present the Democrats enjoy the support of majorities of Latinos and supermajorities of black Americans.[27] This permits the Democrats to champion expansions both of means-tested welfare programs and of universal social insurance—while Republicans attack both versions of the welfare state.

But this situation is unlikely to last. For one thing, as white voters with residual racist attitudes dwindle as a share of the electorate, Republicans who seek to create a more racially inclusive party are likely to succeed in making their party more friendly to racial and religious minorities, undercutting the advantage of the Democrats.

At the same time, the increasing racial liberalism of American society may also lead to greater emphasis on economic divides, rather than racial divisions. The latent tension within the Democratic coalition between the urban poor who depend on means-tested welfare and the suburban working-class and middle-class Americans of all races who make too much money to be eligible for most means-tested anti-poverty programs might turn into a chasm between two transformed parties. If anti-Latino nativism on the right fades, there is no reason to believe that assimilated, middle-class Latinos in a few generations will vote like poor recent immigrants from Latin America in the downtowns of Densitaria rather than like their own non-Latino neighbors who live next door in Posturbia. Instead of a politics of cross-class coalitions within races, a much less racist America might witness the emergence of more important cross-racial coalitions within classes.

5.

It may be that I am mistaken and that none of these scenarios will come to pass. But a political system in which all major variants of public philosophy are represented in both national parties seems unlikely, except in a transitional period. If the triumph of social liberalism does produce a new contest between liberaltarianism and populiberalism, the U.S. is likely to end up with both a predominantly liberaltarian party and a predominantly populiberal one. To be sure, my provocative terms will not be used; the existing terminology of "Left" and "Right," "conservative" and "liberal" (or "progressive") will almost certainly continue to be used, with new meanings. Tomorrow there will be a Left, a Right, and a Center—but the Left, Right and Center of tomorrow will not be those of today.

Notes

1. Robert P. Jones, et al, *A Generation in Transition*, Public Religion Research Institute and Berkley Center for Religion, Peace &World Affairs, Washington, DC, April 19, 2012, http://publicreligion.org/site/wp-content/uploads/2012/04/Millennials-Survey-Report .pdf.

2. Jeffrey M. Jones, "Men, Married, and Southerners Most Likely to Be Gun Owners," Gallup, Washington, DC, February 1, 2013, http://www.gallup.com/poll/160223/men -married-southerners-likely-gun-owners.aspx.

3. Shane Goldmacher, "Poll Finds That Obama's Base Overlaps with Gun-Control Coalition," *National Journal*, January 13, 2013, http://www.nationaljournal.com /congressional-connection/coverage/poll-finds-that-obama-s-base-overlaps-with-gun -control-coalition-20130114.

4. Michael Dimock and Carroll Doherty, "Gun Rights Proponents More Politically Active," Pew Research Center, Washington, DC, January 14, 2013, http://www.people-press.org /files/legacy-pdf/01-14-13 Gun Policy Release.pdf.

5. "Changing Attitudes on Gay Marriage," Pew Research Center, Washington, DC, March 2014, http://features.pewforum.org/same-sex-marriage-attitudes/slide2.php.

6. "Democrats' Edge Among Millenials Slips," Pew Research Center, Washington, DC, February 18, 2010, http://www.pewresearch.org/2010/02/18/democrats-edge-among -millennials-slips.

7. Ibid.

8. Rosie Swash, "Bill Clinton's Sister Souljah Moment Tops Year of Political Controversy," *The Guardian*, June 12, 2011, http://www.theguardian.com/music/2011/jun/13/bill -clinton-sister-souljah.

9. "Changing Attitudes on Gay Marriage."

10. "Democrats' Edge Among Millenials Slips."

11. Eileen Patten and Kim Parker, "A Gender Reversal on Career Aspirations," Pew Research Center, Washington, DC, April 19, 2012, http://www.pewsocialtrends .org/2012/04/19/a-gender-reversal-on-career-aspirations/.

12. Gert Pickel, *Religion Monitor: An International Comparison of Religious Belief*, Bertelsmann Stiftung, Germany, 2013, http://www.bertelsmann-stiftung.de/cps/rde /xbcr/SID-345721E1-09996853/bst_engl/xcms_bst_dms_38081__2.pdf.

13. "'Nones' on the Rise," Pew Research Center, Washington, DC, October 9, 2012, http:// www.pewforum.org/2012/10/09/nones-on-the-rise.

14. "Religion Among Millenials," Pew Research Center, Washington, DC, February 17, 2010, http://www.pewforum.org/2010/02/17/religion-among-the-millennials.

15. "Denominational Affiliation (Overview)," Association of Religious Data Archives, University Park, PA, 2010, http://www.thearda.com/quickstats/qs_102_t.asp.

16. "Millenials in Adulthood," Pew Research Center, Washington, DC, March 7, 2014, http://www.pewsocialtrends.org/2014/03/07/millennials-in-adulthood.

17. "2012 Electoral Map: Barack Obama," PoliticalMaps.org, November 6, 2012, http://politicalmaps.org/2012-electoral-map/.

18. Joel Kotkin, "Houston Rising: Why The Next Great American Cities Aren't What You Think," *Daily Beast*, April 8, 2013, http://www.thedailybeast.com/articles/2013/04/08/houston-rising-why-the-next-great-american-cities-aren-t-what-you-think.html.

19. Robert Frank, "Plutonomics," *The Wealth Report* (blog), Wall Street Journal, January 8, 2007, http://blogs.wsj.com/wealth/2007/01/08/plutonomics.

20. American Fact Finder, US Census Bureau, http://factfinder2.census.gov/faces/nav/jsf/pages/index.xhtml.

21. Michael Grynbaum, "Health Panel Approves Restrictions on Sales of Large Sugary Drinks," *New York Times*, September 13, 2012, http://www.nytimes.com/2012/09/14/nyregion/health-board-approves-bloombergs-soda-ban.html?_r=0.

22. Jim Efstathiou Jr., "Fracking Will Support 1.7 Million Jobs, Study Shows," *Bloomberg Businessweek*, October 23, 2012, http://www.businessweek.com/news/2012-10-23/fracking-will-support-1-dot-7-million-jobs-study-shows.

23. Alex Trembath, et al, *Coal Killer*, Breakthrough Institute, Oakland, CA, June 25, 2013, /images/main_image/Breakthrough_Institute_Coal_Killer.pdf.

24. Jim Snyder, "Ohio's Gas-Fracking Boom Seen Aiding Obama in Swing State," *Bloomberg*, September 4, 2012, https://www.bloomberg.com/news/articles/2012-09-04/ohio-s-gas-fracking-boom-seen-aiding-obama-in-swing-state.

25. Barack Obama, "Remarks by the President on Climate Change" (speech, Georgetown University, Washington, DC, June 25, 2013) http://www.whitehouse.gov/the-press-office/2013/06/25/remarks-president-climate-change.

26. Jesse Jenkins, "The Sherrod Brown Test: Finding Consensus on Climate Policy," *the Breakthrough*, April 23, 2009, http://thebreakthrough.org/archive/the_sherrod_brown_test_finding.

27. Frank Newport, "Democrats Racially Diverse; Republicans Mostly White," Gallup, Princeton, NJ, February 8, 2013, http://www.gallup.com/poll/160373/democrats-racially-diverse-republicans-mostly-white.aspx.

Periodical and Internet Sources Bibliography

*The following articles have been selected to supplement the diverse
views presented in this chapter.*

Alexa Arch, "Identity Politics: The Left's Deceitful Campaign for
    Conformity," *Future Female Leader*, http://futurefemaleleader
    .com/identity-politics-the-lefts-deceitful-campaign-for
    -conformity.

American Spectator, "The Future Of Identity Politics," June 3, 2015,
    https://spectator.org/62934_future-identity-politics.

Tom Ashbrook, "The Future—Or End—Of Identity Politics," WBUR,
    November 23, 2016, http://www.wbur.org/onpoint/2016/11/23
    /identity-politics-clinton-trump-voters.

Jonathan Friedman, "The Past in the Future: History and the Politics
    of Identity," *American Anthropologist*, Vol. 94 No 4 (December
    1992), pp. 837–859.

Eric D. Knowles and Linda R. Tropp, "The Rise of White Identity
    Politics," *New Republic*, October 28, 2016, https://newrepublic
    .com/article/138230/rise-white-identity-politics.

Nicholas Kristoff, "Identity Politics and a Dad's Loss," *New York
    Times*, December 8, 2016, https://www.nytimes.com/2016/12/08
    /opinion/identity-politics-and-a-dads-loss.html.

Mark Lilla, "The End of Identity Liberalism," *New York Times*,
    November 18, 2016, https://www.nytimes.com/2016/11/20
    /opinion/.../the-end-of-identity-liberalism.html.

Leigh Ann Smith, "How to Win With Identity Politics," The
    Establishment, March 29, 2017, https://theestablishment.co/how
    -to-win-with-identity-politics-f8641286b52b.

Eric Stetson, "Identity Politics and the Future of the Democratic Part,"
    Daily Kos, April 27, 2017, https://www.dailykos.com
    /stories/2017/4/27/1656727/-The-Poor-Political-Strategy-of
    -Markos-Moulitsas-and-the-Future-of-the-Democratic-Party.

Heather Wilhelm, "No, The Future Is Not Female," National Review,
    February 8, 2017, http://www.nationalreview.com/article/444699
    /future-is-female-problematic-feminist-slogan.

For Further Discussion

Chapter 1
1. How would you define identity politics?
2. How did identity politics first emerge?
3. What are some historical examples of identity politics? Explain?

Chapter 2
1. What is intersectionality?
2. Are intersectionality and identity politics similar sides to the same coin? Why or why not?
3. Has identity politics failed to incorporate intersectionality? Why or why not?

Chapter 3
1. What is Marxism?
2. Why do many Marxists critique identity politics?
3. Besides social class, what other important aspect of identity do you believe has been left out of identity politics?

Chapter 4
1. Have recent political events shown that identity politics works or do they show that identity politics needs to be reworked?
2. How might identity politics need to be reformed?
3. Will we always rely on some form of identity politics? Why or why not?

Organizations to Contact

The editors have compiled the following list of organizations concerned with the issues debated in this book. The descriptions are derived from materials provided by the organizations. All have publications or information available for interested readers. The list was compiled on the date of publication of the present volume; the information provided here may change. Be aware that many organizations take several weeks or longer to respond to inquiries, so allow as much time as possible.

The Anti-Defamation League (ADL)

605 3rd Avenue
New York, NY 10158
(212) 885-7700
website: www.adl.org

The Anti-Defamation League is one of the earliest American organizations dedicated to social justice. Founded in 1913 to fight against Jewish discrimination, it continues to work toward justice and fair treatment for all individuals.

Foundation for Individual Rights in Education (FIRE)

510 Walnut Street, Suite 1250
Philadelphia, PA 19106
(212) 717-FIRE
website: www.thefire.org

Founded in 1999, FIRE works to secure individual rights on American college campuses. Its mission includes protecting freedom of speech, legal equality, due process, and religious liberty.

The National Association for the Advancement of Colored People (NAACP)

4805 Mt. Hope Drive
Baltimore, MD 21215
(877) NAACP-98
website: www.naacp.org
Twitter: @NAACP

The NAACP is the nation's oldest and largest civil rights organization, founded in 1909. It was founded in response to the horrific practice of lynching in the American South after the end of slavery and continues to fight for the rights of African Americans in the United States.

The National Center for Transgender Equality (NCTE)

1400 16th Street NW, Suite 510
Washington, DC 20036
website: www.transequality.org
202-642-4542
Facebook: @TransEqualityNow
Twitter: @TransEquality

The NCTE was founded in 2003 in order to fight for transgender equality and to ensure policy change that positively affects transgender individuals. The NCTE uses a two-pronged approach, by empowering transgender individuals and their supporters while simultaneously influencing policy makers to ensure trans rights.

National Organization for Women (NOW)

1100 H Street NW, Suite 300
Washington, DC 20005
(202) 628-8NOW
website: www.now.org
Twitter: @nationalNOW

The National Organization for Women was founded in 1966 as the grassroots arm of the women's liberation movement. Today, NOW takes a multistrategy approach to women's rights and is the largest feminist organization in the United States.

Parents, Families, and Friends of Lesbians and Gays (PFLAG)

1828 L Street NW, Suite 660
Washington, DC 20036
(202) 467-8180
website: www.pflag.org
Twitter: @PFLAG

PFLAG was founded in 1972 by a woman who wanted to support her gay son by creating an association to provide support for gay and lesbian individuals, their families, and their supporters. Today, PFLAG has four hundred chapters and over two hundred thousand supporters across the United States.

Southern Poverty Law Center (SPLC)

400 Washington Avenue
Montgomery, AL 36104
(888) 414-7752
website: www.splcenter.org
Facebook: @SPLCenter
Twitter: @SPLCenter

The SPLC was created in 1971 in order to extend the promise of the civil rights movement to all. This important civil rights organization has won significant legal victories in the area of civil rights, which has included fighting against remnants of Jim Crow segregation.

UnidosUS

1126 16th Street NW, Suite 600
Washington, DC 20036
(202) 785-1670
website: www.unidosus.org
Facebook: @WeareUnidosus
Twitter: @WeareUnidosus

Formerly known as NCLR, UnidosUS was founded in 1968 and is one of the largest organizations for Latinos in the United States. The organization serves the Hispanic community through research, policy analysis, and state and national advocacy efforts.

Women's March

Washington, DC
website: www.womensmarch.com
Twitter: @womensmarch

The Women's March Organization was created in late 2016 after Donald Trump's election as US president. Originally a mass movement of protest following Donald Trump's inauguration, the organization has expanded to provide intersectional education, training, outreach programs, and events for grassroots activists and organizers.

Bibliography of Books

Linda Martin Alcoff, *Identity Politics Reconsidered* (Future of Minority Studies). New York, NY: Palgrave Macmillan, 2006.

Bruce Bawer, *The Victims' Revolution: The Rise of Identity Studies and the Closing of the Liberal Mind*. New York, NY: Broadside Books, 2012.

Ian Bremmer, *Us Vs. Them: The Failure of Globalism*. New York, NY: Portfolio, 2018.

Stokely Carmicael and Muia Abu-Jamal, *Stokely Speaks: From Black Power to Pan-Africanism*. Chicago, IL: Chicago Review Press, 2007.

Sheryll Cashin, *Loving: Interracial Intimacy in America and the Threat to White Supremacy*. Boston, MA: Beacon Press, 2017.

Ashley D. Farmer, *Remaking Black Power: How Black Women Transformed an Era* (Justice, Power, and Politics). Chapel Hill, NC: University of North Caroline, 2017.

Nancy Fraser, *The Fortunes of Feminism: From Women's Liberation to Identity Politics to Capitalism to Neoliberal Crisis*. New York, NY: Verso, 2013.

Jonah Goldberg, *Suicide of the West: How the Rebirth of Populism, Nationalism, and Identity Politics Is Destroying American Democracy*. New York, NY: Random House, 2018.

Scott Greer, *No Campus for White Men; The Transformation of Higher Education into Hateful Indoctrination*. Washington, DC: WND Books, 2017.

Asad Haider, *Mistaken Identity: Race and Class in the Age of Trump*. New York, NY: Verso, 2018.

Kim R. Holmes, *The Closing of the Liberal Mind: How Groupthink and Intolerance Define the Left*. Encounter Books, 2017.

Mark Lilla, *The Once and Future Liberal: After Identity Politics*. New York, NY: Harper, 2017.

Cristina Pérez, *Red, White and Latina: Our American Identity*. Morgan James Publishing, 2017.

Barbara Ryan, *Identity Politics in the Women's Movement*. New York, NY: NYU Press, 2001.

Index